UNLOCKING
Wealth

UNLOCKING Wealth

SECRETS TO GETTING RICH AT ANY AGE

ROHIT SARIN

ALEPH

ALEPH BOOK COMPANY
An independent publishing firm
promoted by *Rupa Publications India*

First published in India in 2024
by Aleph Book Company
7/16 Ansari Road, Daryaganj
New Delhi 110 002

Copyright © Rohit Sarin 2024

All rights reserved.

The author has asserted his moral rights.

The views and opinions expressed in this book are the author's own and the facts are as reported by him, which have been verified to the extent possible, and the publishers are not in any way liable for the same.

The publisher has used its best endeavours to ensure that URLs for external websites referred to in this book are correct and active at the time of going to press. However, the publisher has no responsibility for the websites and can make no guarantee that a site will remain live or that the content is or will remain appropriate.

No part of this publication may be reproduced, transmitted, or stored in a retrieval system, in any form or by any means, without permission in writing from Aleph Book Company.

ISBN: 978-81-19635-49-8

1 3 5 7 9 10 8 6 4 2

Printed in India

This book is sold subject to the condition that it shall not, by way of trade or otherwise, be lent, resold, hired out, or otherwise circulated without the publisher's prior consent in any form of binding or cover other than that in which it is published.

For
My parents Uma & Sushil Sarin who gave me the values
Meeta who gave me the vision
Naina & Nandini who keep inspiring me
Milo who is our bundle of joy

∞

CONTENTS

Introduction ix

Part I
Why Wealth?

1. Why is Wealth Creation Important for Society? 3
2. Why is Wealth Creation Important for Every Individual? 14

Part II
Laws of Creating Wealth

3. The Recipe for Wealth Creation 27
4. Adding Value by Solving a Problem 36
5. Hunger Versus Greed 50
6. Input Versus Output 63
7. Purpose Versus Numbers 71
8. Risk-taking 81
9. Compounding Effect 91
10. Learning from Failing and Succeeding 103
11. Showing Up in Life 113

Part III
Laws of Managing Wealth

12. What to Do to Retain Wealth? 127
13. Protecting and Growing 136
14. Expenses and Lifestyle Management 147
15. Ego Versus Self-respect 158

16. Depreciating Versus Appreciating Assets — 170
17. Compounding Effect Revisited — 180
18. Importance of Financial Advice — 190

Conclusion: A Quick Guide to the Laws
of Creating, Protecting, and Growing Wealth — 199
Acknowledgements — 203
References — 205

INTRODUCTION

India is on the cusp of becoming the world's third largest economy. In fact, if India's GDP continues to grow at over 7 per cent every year (add to that inflation of 4 per cent plus every year), then India's current GDP, which has crossed US$ 4 trillion (₹332 lakh crore), is expected to grow three times in rupee terms[*] over next ten years. If that happens, then every business in India, big and small, if managed well, could grow at least five times, if not more, over the next ten years. Once that happens India will be on its way to becoming a developed nation over the next twenty-five years. Indians, who account for 20 per cent of the humanity on this planet, will become the biggest consumer market of the world. In this context, there is no better time for the growth of wealth consciousness among us Indians. We should look to build wealth in order to uplift ourselves individually as well as the nation as a whole.

Especially in the Indian context, wanting to build wealth is often seen as an undesirable trait, a symptom of greed. But it is not only a requirement to afford individual needs such as food, clothing, shelter, education, healthcare, it is also essential to be able to live a life of comfort and dignity. Societies and nations also need to make wealth to be able to provide amenities to their citizens. So while greed and exploitation should be

---

[*]On account of the rupee dollar depreciation of around 3% per annum in dollar terms, the economy may grow around 2.3 times over ten years but in rupee terms it will grow three times.

avoided, the building of wealth is a critically important goal for any society that wishes to improve the quality of life of its people.

There are various ways in which people can build wealth (and we will discuss this through the book)—they can earn through their professional careers, by starting a business that addresses a lack or solves a problem, by investing in a variety of instruments such as equity, debt, real estate, gold, etc. But before putting money into assets that are meant to grow wealth, one must have a fundamental understanding of wealth, how it can be grown, what it means for individuals and societies to build wealth and how to avoid the risks associated with wealth creation.

This book endeavours to demystify the process of wealth creation. Rather than a templated roadmap based on micro rules for managing expenses and investments, it offers a vision document. This is not a self-help book to get rich. Neither is it a rule-based guide to achieve financial freedom. Rather it is a lucid introduction to the world of wealth, encouraging and enabling its readers to become wealth creators based entirely on real-life learnings from a practitioner.

My understanding of wealth creation comes from my own journey of twenty-five years as a wealth manager, which began in February 1999. I was hired by a multinational bank as part of its start-up team to launch their wealth management business in India. Those were early days for the concept of wealth management in India when wealth belonged to a limited set of privileged families which were largely generational business owners. Wealth creation for everyone else was limited and the bug of entrepreneurship was yet to be unleashed. This has changed over the last quarter century and I have been privileged to witness the wealth effect that has transformed

Indian society. As a student of wealth, I have learnt on the job about the phenomenon of wealth creation as well as its erosion. Having worked very closely with India's wealth owners and creators, I have observed at close quarters what works and, more importantly, what doesn't work when it comes to the matter of wealth. In this book, I share the lessons I have picked up on my journey.

The book is in three parts. Part I: Why Wealth? explains why wealth creation is important and why it should be a key life goal for every individual. Part II: Laws of Wealth Creation demystifies the process of wealth creation by sharing nuggets of practical wisdom learnt from my experience as a wealth practitioner to enable every reader to become a wealth creator. Part III: Laws of Managing Wealth shows how to keep the wealth once it has been created.

Through this book, I hope that readers will come to a better understanding of how wealth can be created, secured, and grown to be able to lead the lives they want and to contribute to the upliftment and betterment of society.

PART I

WHY WEALTH?

Chapter 1

WHY IS WEALTH CREATION IMPORTANT FOR SOCIETY?

Affluent societies can take better care of their citizens and this makes the world a better place.

Wealth is the engine of the world. Having wealth leads to a virtuous cycle of affluence for societies and nations since wealth creates more wealth. Absence of wealth condemns the society to a vicious cycle of impoverishment, weighing down the human potential.

Wealth is the resource that ensures the desired quality of life and plays a critical role in harnessing, at the macro level, a country's true potential. Affluence helps societies provide those living in it access to the best education and healthcare. It enables faster mobility, whether physical or virtual. Affluence also leads to greater affordability, which creates demand for products and services, thereby creating entrepreneurial and business opportunities, which in turn creates jobs. Wealth is, therefore, the catalyst that creates livelihoods.

It will be fair to say, in light of the above, that wealth is the enabler for making the world a better place. It is also the life force behind national, social, and individual well-being. The history of the last half a century alone will show that nations and societies that do not create wealth or deliberately ignore or look down upon those who create it invariably atrophy, fall behind those that do and, in many cases, even splinter and break up. A glance at the recent histories of Eastern European Communist countries, Cuba, and others will prove this point. These countries shut themselves to the world and missed out on participating in the globalization of the world economy.

The equation is simple. If a pool of wealth is wisely and efficiently deployed, it will multiply and create more wealth. This will help spread the circle of prosperity by bringing more people within its ambit. And this, in turn, will result in a more educated workforce that has access to better healthcare and improve the quality of life of a greater number of people. This virtuous cycle will keep expanding, benefitting more and more people as long as society keeps generating wealth.

Wealth creation must, therefore, be a critically important goal for any society that wishes to improve the quality of life of its people as it fosters economic growth, which is the basic building block of any society. Governments that encourage economic growth succeed in creating jobs for their citizens, providing better governance, and creating improved physical and social infrastructure that support vibrant, productive populations that can focus on reaching their full potential in their chosen field of activity.

No society is hundred percent egalitarian and equal because no two human beings are the same. Even prosperous and harmonious societies, therefore, have some level of inequality and poverty. However, societies that create wealth are usually more successful in alleviating poverty than those that do not create wealth. Wealth creation, therefore, plays a critical part in combating poverty.

Most governments try to provide high quality education, world-class medical facilities, a pollution-free environment, and clean and safe neighbourhoods to their citizens. These cost a lot of money to set up and maintain. The fuel that keeps this social infrastructure running is wealth, and societies that create wealth are best equipped to carry on enjoying high quality lives.

Along with public services, governments are also mandated to provide good physical infrastructure such as roads, power, telecoms, transportation, etc., which are essential for growth. You will see that societies that are prosperous are also usually better endowed with such infrastructure. The reason is simple: the wealth that they create goes into building this infrastructure.

Economic growth, the provision of public services like healthcare and education, the building of public infrastructure like roads, railways, and airports, and other such activities create opportunities for entrepreneurship and employment. This draws larger numbers of people into the expanding circle of prosperity, spurs consumer demand for a range of products and services, and lays the foundation for the next round of economic expansion and therefore job creation.

A society's search for newer, more efficient, and cheaper products encourages innovation and this results in technological breakthroughs that lead to radical new capabilities being developed. These expand the horizons of science and result in an exponential improvement in human knowledge and productivity. The fuel that enables this evolution through innovation is wealth.

DEFINING WEALTH

Wealth is a societal resource that helps run the world. It may manifest in various forms—as currency which helps to transact and as capital—one of the three factors of economic production other than labour and land and the enterprise value of a business, goodwill of a brand, patents or physical assets like real estate and gold. It makes things happen, moving people from one place to another, transporting goods from one country to another, delivering products from factories to consumers, and providing people with the wherewithal to lead better lives and reach their full potential.

This makes wealth the key driver of productivity of people, institutions, governments, and entire economies. Although it is fashionable in some circles to downplay the critical role of wealth in the life of a nation, the entire system of governance will break down if society stops generating wealth. Wealth is the resource needed by the governments to run their countries. Any government can become dysfunctional in the absence of an approved budget. In that light, wealth enables governance in the world.

WEALTH AS A DETERMINANT OF HISTORY

Wealth has always played a key role in shaping events throughout history. All kingdoms and empires were founded and built in the pursuit of wealth. The history of colonization, which has had a deep and pervasive influence on almost every country in the world, was the story of the pursuit of wealth. Relatively smaller European nations succeeded in conquering and colonizing much bigger countries with much larger populations only because the former were creating more wealth by providing better education to their citizens, which enabled them to stay ahead of the innovation curve for several centuries. They allowed them to build bigger navies and better firearms facilitating their emergence as dominant military powers.

The outcome of the Cold War was also decided not by the power of arms but by the relative economic health of the opposing sides. The US-led western bloc managed to innovate and create better technologies than the Soviet Union and its allies because the former were more efficient wealth creators, while the latter, weighed down by an ideology that scorned wealth creation fell behind in the innovation and economic race till it could compete no further.

Let's consider the examples of West Germany and East Germany and North Korea and South Korea. As everyone knows, West Germany chose to remain on the free market path and, despite being flattened to rubble by the end of World War II, rose like a phoenix within a few decades and became the economic powerhouse of western Europe. East Germany, on the other hand, was almost bankrupt and on the verge of economic collapse after four decades of Communist rule when the two parts of the country reunited.

It is the same story in the case of the two Koreas. Despite having several natural advantages, North Korea has fallen behind, while South Korea has pulled itself from near destitution to First World status by relentlessly pursuing the path of wealth creation. As a result, it is now one of the world's most educated and innovative societies and leads the comity of nations in high technology fields such as electronics, automobiles, and shipbuilding, among others.

Closer home, India's own example will suffice to highlight the importance of wealth creation in the life of a country. From Independence till 1991, the Indian political elite exhibited a marked disdain for the creation of wealth and disparaged the important role of wealth creators in nation building. Those who have memories of that era will remember it as the age of shoddy, outdated goods, shortages, black marketing, and smuggling. It was little wonder then that a philosophy that looked down upon wealth creation led the country to the brink of bankruptcy in 1991.

The economic liberalization programme unveiled by then Prime Minister P. V. Narasimha Rao and his economic team led by then Finance Minister Dr Manmohan Singh in 1991 changed the economic trajectory of the country and transformed it from a poor Third World nation struggling to make ends meet to the toast of global corner offices. The fuel for this turbo-charged transformation was wealth creation.

Today, Indian companies—owned by both domestic as well as foreign investors—are at the cutting edge of global innovation and creating wealth in diverse sectors such as software, electronics, pharmaceuticals, automobiles, financial services, and a host of others.

Almost every Fortune 500 company has a presence in India. And the country features prominently in all economic, diplomatic, and geostrategic discussions anywhere in the world. The primary reason for this change of perception about India is that the country has begun to realize its potential as a creator of wealth for itself and the world.

WEALTH CREATORS ARE THE NEW STARS

Businesses that create wealth are the darlings of investors. Deep pocketed international and domestic investors are falling over themselves to get a piece of the action in Indian business houses such as Reliance Industries, Tata Group, Infosys, and Aditya Birla Group, among others.

On the other hand, public sector companies such as HMT and Allwyn, which were market leaders in the wrist watches and refrigerator industries in an earlier era, have had to be shuttered and in some cases sold following sustained losses over many years. Then, India's flagship airline Air India had to be sold back to its original promoter, the Tata Group, after incurring heavy losses for many years. The reason: these PSUs made inefficient capital allocation decisions that led to erosion of their enterprise value. The result: they were not able to create wealth.

WEALTH CREATION DRIVES PROGRESS

Thus, we see that wealth is the essential fuel that is needed to keep the wheels of countries, societies, and corporations moving. Whenever there is a let up in the process of wealth creation, the institution—whether countries, blocs, or companies—and its stakeholders suffer setbacks. If the process of wealth creation stops for an extended period, it could signal the end of the road for the entities involved.

Thus, wealth creation is the most important driver of progress and well-being at the global, national, and societal levels.

In its most fundamental sense, wealth is a multifaceted resource that powers the engine of societies, nations, and the entire world. It will be wrong to see it only in terms of the material concept, since it is much more than the mere accumulation of valuable assets that most people suggest it is.

Rather, it should be defined as a dynamic concept that is the sum of the financial value of underlying assets along with the potential for future realization of value from such assets and the opportunities they create for individuals and societies.

ROLE OF WEALTH IN THE MODERN WORLD

The primary role of wealth is to facilitate the expansion of economies and create a more prosperous world, as we've seen. An expanding economy that is well governed creates greater opportunities for all its constituents. These 'benefits' include not only economic rewards but also access to better education, medical facilities, sanitation, governance, law and order, and public infrastructure. This helps bridge the gap between the haves and have nots and create more egalitarian societies. One must add here that good governance is a prerequisite for such egalitarian development. Its absence can lead to rising inequality and result in social tensions.

The history of western Europe and Southeast Asia shows us that wealth creation across the board—and across an entire region—can lead to a prolonged period of peace and prosperity. Both these regions were theatres of major conflicts and bloodshed for several centuries up to the end of World War II. The unprecedented wealth created by countries in these regions since then has coincided with seven decades of peace and prosperity.

On the other hand, regions that are marked by economic downturns and the absence of wealth creation often see conflicts and wars. There are dozens of examples of countries—Venezuela, Columbia, Argentina, Niger, Burkina Faso, Chad, Sudan—endowed with great material resources remaining poor as they have not been able to harness their wealth for the benefit of their citizens.

In times of slowdowns, even progressive economies become inward looking and clamp down on imports and external trade. This can lead to a vicious cycle of ever lower levels of wealth creation and a dilution in the quality of life of people in that society. This also weakens linkages already created between societies and individuals and can lead to isolationism, protectionism, and further economic contraction.

Sports offers excellent examples of how wealth helps unleash the full potential of human achievement. Although there are some honourable exceptions, you will observe that a majority of the world's leading sportspersons hail from affluent countries. That is because excelling in sports requires access to world-class coaching, equipment, infrastructure, and participation in globally competitive events. All of this requires substantial investment, which only affluent nations can afford. It's clear that India has come to dominate the cricketing world on account of the humungous wealth creation unleased by the IPL format (we will look at this issue in greater detail in Chapter 2).

WEALTH HELPS MAKE THE WORLD A BETTER PLACE

Wealth is an enabler that helps create a better world. Seventy years ago, only Europe, the USA, and a few other mainly white countries were considered 'developed'. The rest of the world was called 'developing' or 'underdeveloped'. The creation of wealth by many more countries across the world means those distinctions are now much less sharp in several parts of Asia. Singapore, Hong Kong, Taiwan, and South Korea, all hubs of wealth creation, are now classified as 'developed', while most other countries are upper-middle and middle-income states, with dramatic improvements in governance, law and order, and the quality of lives of their citizens. People in these countries, including in India, can spend more money on things they want, invest in bigger homes, travel more often, and buy more discretionary goods. This creates a virtuous cycle of growth and prosperity that we discussed above.

Then, leveraging and reinvesting wealth creates more wealth. These countries have invested their wealth wisely—in creating social and physical infrastructure and providing better governance and security to their citizens. These investments lead to more investments, create jobs, demand for various goods and services, and creates a cycle of affluence. This transformation has been made possible by one critical factor—the creation of wealth.

Exactly the opposite has happened in the case of Pakistan (in 2023) and Sri Lanka (in 2022). Poor economic management and reckless fiscal measures combined to bankrupt their exchequers. With no money to pay for essential imports and very little fuel in their inventories, both countries virtually came to a standstill. The inability of these countries to create wealth is killing the potential of their citizens to lead fulfilling lives and condemning them to lives of poverty. Massive infusions of external aid—from India in the case of Sri Lanka and Saudi Arabia, UAE, and China in the case of Pakistan—followed by aid from the International Monetary Fund (IMF) have helped restart their stalled economies but both remain in ICU with no hope of any major improvement in their health in the short to medium terms. In that sense, these countries are in the same boat as companies that have become bankrupt.

WEALTH IS THE REAL FUEL

You need petrol, diesel, and now a charged battery to drive your car. If you do not have fuel, your car will not move, and you will be rendered immobile. It is exactly the same with countries and societies.

Creating wealth and generating surpluses should, therefore, be considered a mandatory obligation of every member of society. As we have seen above, this can be in the form of currency, capital, equity in business, infrastructure, the imparting of knowledge, or the dispensing of critical services in the healthcare and other domains, but wealth creation is sine qua non for any society to grow and prosper.

There is, therefore, absolutely no shame in being a wealth creator because that is the both the fuel and the engine that propels all progress. It is the foundational resource of modern life; the world as we know it will not survive if we do not create adequate wealth to invest in the next round of growth.

Chapter 2

WHY IS WEALTH CREATION IMPORTANT FOR EVERY INDIVIDUAL?

Wealth enables an individual to celebrate life and become an inspiring catalyst for spreading prosperity.

In the previous chapter, we discussed why wealth creation is a critical social good and how it keeps the wheels of society greased and turning. Building on that argument, this chapter will explain the importance of wealth as the engine for every individual.

The larger goal of every individual is to achieve lasting happiness, which is possible only if he/she can achieve peace with prosperity. One needs both to make life meaningful and complete. For every individual, wealth is a means to an end, which is to celebrate life. Beyond meeting immediate material objectives, wealth gives an individual the freedom to live the life of one's choice. These choices could range from consumption (i.e. basic requirements) to lifestyle (the extras). If one has more wealth than is needed to fund these choices, then individuals can share a part of their wealth with those who need it. Wealth distribution in society is possible only if there is wealth creation.

While consumption needs are usually finite, the goal of giving away is limitless. Similarly, all that one needs for achieving a high quality of life is also finite but wants can be infinite. Therefore, wealth creation should be the lifetime goal of every individual and shouldn't be limited to retirement planning.

THE MEANING OF WEALTH AND ITS IMPORTANCE FOR INDIVIDUALS

At the level of the individual, wealth addresses one's immediate financial, social, emotional, and material needs and then gives flexibility to satisfy one's wants—which can be defined as those discretionary items that may not be absolutely necessary, but which satisfy some craving or desire.

People strive to create wealth for a number of reasons. The most common ones are:

1. Financial security
2. Access to better quality of life
3. Unleashing an individual's potential
4. Leaving a legacy for future generations
5. Giving back to society
6. Social mobility, acceptance, and prestige

In addition, wealth plays a pivotal role in giving access to a life with freedom of time. Wealth therefore is the fuel for an individual to live life to the fullest and leave behind a world richer than the one he/she inherited.

It is natural for every individual to want to earn more money and accumulate more wealth than he/she needs in order to save for the future. Over a period, this corpus could grow to a substantial amount. It could then be deployed to provide for one's old age, children's education, acquisition of assets for personal use like a home or car or be used to fund holidays and other consumption needs. The ability to provide for all of these and other expenses provides us with financial security. As an extension of this, wealth can also be deployed to improve one's quality of life. For example, one can buy a bigger home, a better car, employ staff to help out with daily work, buy a holiday home in a hill station to escape the noise, grime, and pollution of big cities, fund children's education in the best institutions, access high quality healthcare, and indulge in leisure activities that remain out of reach for those without adequate purchasing power.

Wealth also plays a critical role in giving an individual the freedom of exercising his/her choices. It also provides the wealth owner the flexibility of when and how to exercise these choices. Wealth is the fuel that opens up opportunities in line with an individual's inclinations and tastes and provides the option to pursue his/her desired goals—be it in terms of career choices, hobbies, travel destinations, food preferences, or in the exercise of any other personal choices. Wealth also gives individuals the option to decide important things like where they live, what they do, how and where they spend their hours of leisure, and take decisions that align with their life's goals and desires. It, therefore, gives people the option to exercise their discretion without any constraints or fear. It is also a critical factor in enabling an individual to achieve a balance between professional goals and financial requirements on the one hand and intangible but necessary benefits such as time for building emotional bonds with people, pets, and passions, spending time and effort on interpersonal relationships, and focusing attention on personal development objectives on the other.

Then, wealth also plays a major role in increasing a person's self-esteem and confidence. This directly contradicts what many of us are taught from childhood. In many families, children are indoctrinated from an early age to believe that wealth does not, should not, and cannot define the self-worth of an individual. This becomes an article of faith, which then clashes with the realities of life when these children come face to face with everyday situations. Shorn of ideology and hypocrisy, the truth is that wealth plays a very important—and often the most critical—role in defining an individual's self-esteem, self-worth, and self-development. It can give a sense of accomplishment to an individual, provide validation of one's enterprise, and convert one's dreams into reality. As a resource, it helps the individual unleash his true potential by getting access to world class education, coaching, platforms, and networks.

Wealth also provides the ballast for social mobility. The most striking examples of this can be found among successful start-up entrepreneurs and executives. Many young men and women from ordinary backgrounds have become household names within a short time because of their success in creating wealth for themselves and their investors.

Having wealth gives people the means to provide for their families and their future generations. This allows the next generation to have a head start over others and access the best education, healthcare, and leisure facilities that would remain out of reach in the absence of their inter-generational wealth. This can be a massive source of comfort for the wealth creator—to know that his/her children and their progeny are well provided for.

Many wealthy individuals set up trusts, foundations, and endowments to give back to the society in diverse fields such as health, education, geriatric care, women and child welfare, environment, sanitation, poverty eradication, etc. These charitable and philanthropic activities have a positive social impact and make a material difference to the world. Globally, the examples of Rockefeller Foundation, Ford Foundation, and the Bill and Melinda Gates Foundation shine through. Closer home, we have the Tata Trusts, the Azim Premji Foundation, the Shiv Nadar Foundation, and innumerable charities set up by wealth creators such as Mukesh Ambani, Nandan Nilekani, among others, which are making a huge difference to the lives of millions of beneficiaries. And wealth is the fuel that powers these charities.

WEALTH EQUALS FLEXIBILITY

As we have discussed earlier, wealth also gives people flexibility over time and choices in life. This allows an individual to pursue interests and passions on which he/she is not dependent for funding one's lifestyle and gives people greater freedom to express themselves in various ways. Access to wealth is one of the most important ways to give a person control over his/her life.

Let us take three examples to illustrate this point. A daily wage earner such as a farm labourer, or a construction worker, or a rickshaw puller lives by the day. If this individual does not find work on a particular day, it is quite likely that he/she and his/her dependents may have to go hungry that day. If such joblessness persists for a few days, the very survival of that family will come into question. The unfortunate but harsh reality is that such a person/family is at a subsistence level of survival and lives, very often, at the margins of society. This individual has limited choices in life beyond securing his daily needs.

Our next examples are those of two individuals holding day jobs—defined as regular employment that keeps them occupied five or six days a week and gives them a salary at the end of the month. One of them is an office boy and the other is a senior manager. Obviously, they live at different levels of the financial and social spectrum. The similarities—full-time jobs in the same organization and salaries at the end of the month—are superficial. The differences in their stations in life are more real. Though both use their salaries to pay bills, educate their children, and save for the future, the senior manager obviously has many more choices and greater flexibility available than either the office boy or the daily wager in the previous example.

For example, having a bigger, better, higher paying job allows the senior manager to live in an affluent and safe neighbourhood, have personal transport, send his children to better schools, and go on holidays more often than his office boy colleague. This means that the senior manager and his/her family have many more options and choices available to them than people lower down the wealth ladder.

Our next example is that of a successful business owner. Obviously, this individual belongs to a separate category of wealth creators altogether and has the maximum flexibility and freedom to pursue his/her dreams and ambitions because his choices in life are not constrained by his monthly pay cheque.

In the above examples, it is only the different levels of wealth that gives these individuals varying degrees of autonomy. They are both enabled and restricted by the different levels of their wealth to pursue their dreams and aspirations.

Wealth is, thus, a means to an end. The goal of most rational human beings is to celebrate life and satisfying one's needs, wants, and desires, and finding a way to fulfil one's aspirations is the way to do it. Wealth is the key to reaching all those goals.

WEALTH AS AN ENABLER

As we have seen in the above passages, wealth is a key facilitator in life and provides several material and psychological advantages to people who possess it and/or know how to create it.

It empowers individuals to overcome the restrictions and obstacles that people face in their lives. It enables people to acquire key skills or desirable objects and enlarges the canvas of a person's life by several multiples.

HOW WEALTH EMPOWERED INDIAN SPORTSPERSONS

Let us take two sets of examples to illustrate this point. It is a common refrain in India that cricket is a religion that unites the entire country. Leading Indian cricketers like Sachin Tendulkar, M. S. Dhoni, Virat Kohli, and others are superstars in every sense of the word and rival the top stars of the film world in popularity, fan following, and wealth.

All the leading Indian cricketers of the last two decades are multi-millionaires several times over. Many of them own multiple homes across different cities in India and abroad, a few of them own private planes, and all of them have large investment portfolios that are expected to generate handsome returns and take care of them in the post-retirement years.

Sponsorships and brand endorsements are their main sources of income, and it is the wealth they generate during their playing years that enables them to focus on their game free from worries about the future. It is this wealth that allows them to maintain a laser focus on their game without having to worry about holding a day job to support themselves and their families and this could be one reason for India emerging as a more formidable cricketing team than at any time in the past.

The same is also true of other disciplines. In recent decades, India's performance in several other sports—such as badminton, javelin throwing, chess, wrestling, boxing, shooting, etc.—have improved quite dramatically. This is evident from the number of individual and team medals that Indian athletes and sportspersons win at global competitions. Corporate sponsorships that have made sports a lucrative calling for successful athletes is a key reason for this transformation in the fortune of Indian sports.

For comparison, let us look back to an earlier era in Indian sports. Our cricketers from the 1980s and earlier were also very talented, but there was little money in the game then and many players needed jobs with public sector banks or private companies to support themselves. Most of them needed these jobs after retiring from the game to lead dignified lives. Notably, no Indian cricket team of the past has attained and sustained the peaks of the current generations of cricketers. And wealth has been a key enabler of this transformation.

The same story repeats itself in other sports. While cricketers of an earlier generation could at least look forward to public sector jobs, athletes in less popular sports often had to live in penury during and after their playing careers.

SCHOLARSHIPS HELP UNLOCK THE POTENTIAL OF MERITORIOUS STUDENTS

Do you know that Dr B. R. Ambedkar, the Father of the Indian Constitution, was awarded a scholarship to pursue his MA at Columbia University? Do you also know that Dr Montek Singh Ahluwalia, who played a key role in India's economic rejuvenation in the post-1991 period, studied on a Rhodes scholarship? Former President of India K. R. Narayanan, nuclear scientist Dr Raja Ramanna, Titan founder Xerxes Desai are among dozens of eminent Indians who could pursue their educational dreams thanks to the J. N. Tata Scholarship. The key enabler in their development was the benevolence of wealth creators.

If these scholarships—and others like them—had not been available, it is quite possible that the world would have been denied some facets of the genius of these individuals. Thus, it will not be wrong to say wealth creators played an important, albeit silent and behind-the-scenes, role in shaping the intellect of these great men and therefore the destinies of the institutions and people that they went on to lead.

There are thousands of other examples of meritorious students who would have stagnated but for the provision of scholarships at key moments of their pedagogical journeys.

THE MULTIPLIER EFFECT

There is a significant stream of thought in India that looks down upon consumption and wealth creation. This is ideological hogwash totally divorced from economic logic. The truth is that in economic theory all consumption is good because it has a multiplier effect and generates several times the wealth than an individual expends on his/her consumption.

When you lead an affluent life, you buy things that provide ballast to the larger economy. For example, when you buy a car, you provide employment not only to the people at the car manufacturer who assemble the vehicle but also in the steel plant, the battery maker, the light company, the leather workers who stitch the seats, the executives in the bank who process the loan and the security guards at the showroom.

This holds true for all expenditure. One person's expense is another person's income. Therefore, whenever a wealthy person spends money, he/she is creating income for the person he buys goods and services from. It, therefore, follows that all consumption generates secondary demand, creates jobs in sectors downstream and upstream of the one in which the primary expenditure is made, and helps spread the virtuous cycle of prosperity in ever expanding waves of concentric circles.

Therefore, individual wealth and wealth creation plays a critical role in spreading prosperity across ever wider swathes of society. For example, a wealthy individual could positively impact the world in the following ways:

1. He could initiate the virtuous cycle of affluence using his wealth to create demand for various products and services to meet his lifestyle requirements.
2. Wealth creating individuals are also performers in the society in their respective domains. A successful entrepreneur, investor, business owner, senior executive, sportsperson, actor, or musician often inspires society and raises the bar of aspirations and performance. Sachin Tendulkar inspired a whole generation of younger cricketers like M. S. Dhoni and Virat Kohli who had grown up watching him become the God of Indian Cricket. Bill Gates, Steve Jobs, Jeff Bezos, and Elon Musk have inspired the entire entrepreneurial ecosystem to think out of the box and solve many problems for the society. Amitabh Bachchan and Shah Rukh Khan have been inspirations for a generation of actors to attempt to make a mark in Bollywood without a godfather.

Warren Buffet has been an inspiration for millions of investors for over more than half a century.
3. Only if you have wealth can you share it. Many a wealthy individual shares part of his/her wealth with those who need it the most, thus creating a lasting impact on society.
4. By leaving a legacy for the family, a wealthy individual provides access to wealth over generations and by virtue of that leaves behind a virtuous cycle of wealth creation in perpetuity.

A wealthy individual, therefore, helps lift the entire society both directly with his wealth and indirectly by becoming a role model for millions of potential wealth creators.

PART II
LAWS OF CREATING WEALTH

Chapter 3

THE RECIPE FOR WEALTH CREATION

Everyone can be a wealth creator. Every wealthy person needn't be a wealth creator. Laws of wealth creation define the path towards wealth creation.

Wealth creation has always been aspirational for the masses. Following the unshackling of the Indian economy in 1991 from stifling and irrational ideological fetters that had held it back in earlier decades, more and more ordinary people are discovering that they, too, can be wealth creators—for themselves, their families, and society.

More than three decades of exposure to the free market has taught us that like everything else we see in the world around us, wealth creation, too, is an output of some input. One can be born rich but, remember, no one is born a wealth creator. Everyone who has created wealth—whether they began their journey with an inheritance or started from nothing—has begun with the seed of an idea. The journey from concept to cash flow and then cash surplus leads to wealth creation.

The pursuit of financial success is now considered a legitimate and desirable goal in life—corresponding to the second stage of life in Indian philosophy where the pursuit of artha (material wealth) and worldly pleasures are considered ideal. In their endeavour to earn and accumulate more wealth, people look for but lack proper guidance on how to reach their goal of becoming wealth creators.

At the outset, it is important to clarify a conceptual confusion in the minds of many people. There is a great deal of difference between being wealthy and being a wealth creator. This is a critical definitional difference that readers must always keep in mind. We will address this issue and several others related to it in the following pages.

THE DIFFERENCE BETWEEN BEING WEALTHY AND BEING A WEALTH CREATOR

Most wealth creators are also very wealthy individuals but not all wealthy persons are wealth creators. The main difference between the two lies in their approach to wealth and their mindset. A wealthy individual may possess substantial assets—financial or physical—either inherited or self-earned. He/she may manage some of these assets on his/her own or may outsource their management to experts or may follow a hybrid model somewhere between these two.

Please note, however, that the wealthy individual referred to above cannot be called a wealth creator if he is not growing his inherited wealth but rather living off the income from the same.

This is because his activities are not enlarging the pool of wealth inherited or created by him in the past. The wealth is simply in maintenance mode and will only keep pace with inflation since the intention of the owner is only to protect the purchasing power of his wealth instead of growing it. This has a cascading effect on wealth creation in society at large since we have learnt in the previous chapters that wealth creates wealth when it moves from one individual to another, one corporation to another, and one country to another.

A wealth creator, on the other hand, is one who enlarges the pool of wealth owned by him since he is growth oriented and, by virtue of that, contributes to the growth of affluence in society as manifested in the growth of its GDP. One simple example of this is an investor in fixed deposit/bond/commercial real estate could be wealthy but not a wealth creator whereas an investor in growth asset classes like listed equities and private equity is likely to be a wealth creator.

Wealth creators play an active role in growing their wealth by maximizing returns on their wealth. Unlike in the example cited above, they are involved in the entire gamut of their business activities from ideation to implementation to marketing and cash flows. They typically put in long hours of hard labour, invest deep thought and introspection, take risks and calculated gambles, network with people who can influence their business outcomes, and remain engaged with their ventures 24x7x365. They must also be prescient and be able to spot new trends ahead of others and be nimble footed enough to be able to benefit from their foresight and their ability to see the future.

One must also note that all wealth creators were not necessarily wealthy to begin with, although they do get to accumulate lots of it over time. There are dozens of examples of people who started with nothing and went on to become billionaires. Bill Gates, Mark Zuckerberg, Larry Ellison, Sergey Brin, and Jack Ma are some of the global examples that come to mind immediately. Closer home, we have the likes of Dhirubhai Ambani, Nikhil Kamath, Nithin Kamath, Sachin Bansal, Binny Bansal, Falguni Nayar, Sanjeev Bikhchandani, Ashish Dhawan, N.R. Narayana Murthy, and Nandan Nilekani, among hundreds of others, who had modest beginnings but dared to dream and went on to found billion-dollar enterprises. Along the way, they not only earned massive fortunes for themselves but also enriched thousands of other stakeholders—employees, shareholders, vendors, customers, and society at large—thus, creating ever widening rings of prosperity and benefitting society as a direct outcome of their personal success.

It will be evident from the above that a proactive approach plays a key role in the process of wealth creation. Most wealth creators are risk takers and innovators who are also good with people having the ability to bring out the best in their teams. They must be focussed and driven by a larger purpose beyond wealth creation while being adaptive to changing environments at the same time.

Wealth creators must also be able to take failures and disappointments in their stride and have the resilience to overcome setbacks that invariably befall every successful entrepreneur. Most importantly, they must have the hunger and ambition to strive for more success at every step of their journey.

These are character traits that anyone can possess. So, it is not true that an inheritor cannot be a wealth creator. The former can become a wealth creator by actively and successfully managing his/her resources. Any individual with hunger, hard work, diligence, innovation, and risk-taking ability can become a wealth creator over a period of time. The distinction between the two is seldom fixed and can alter with time depending on the person's circumstances, mindset, and deeds.

YOU CAN BE A WEALTH CREATOR, TOO

The Indian economy today offers ambitious young (and not so young) people a wide choice of avenues to become wealth creators if they wish to follow that path. Unlike in the past, when wealth was the preserve of a closed club of a select few, the opportunities offered by the spread of technology and education has led to a democratization of the process of wealth creation, bringing it within the reach of the masses. Though people with inherited wealth start with a distinct advantage over those who do not have inter-generational wealth, the process of wealth creation is no longer a function solely of inherited privileges, connections, and customs. Thanks to the plethora of opportunities that abound, anyone with hunger, diligence, perseverance, foresight, and skill can become a wealth creator and, over time, gain a lead over those who began their journeys as inheritors.

Never mind if you are starting from nothing. It does not matter if you are a first-generation entrepreneur. It also matters little if your first or your second or third venture has failed. You can become a successful wealth creator by equipping yourself with the right skills and knowledge, adapting to the vagaries of circumstances, making optimal use of whatever resources you have at your command and the hunger to reach your goal.

It is not necessary to be lucky to become a wealth creator. While fate determines the family, society, or country we are born into, we create our destiny driven by the actions that we take in our life. Destiny is created by any individual driven by the conscious choice of the destination we want to reach in life and what we do in our lifetime to get there. Instead of being constrained by where we are today, being driven by where we can be tomorrow will lead to wealth creation.

So, it is not necessary to be born into a business family to succeed as an entrepreneur. Anyone from any background can attain success in business—and there are enough examples to prove this.

INHERITORS AS WEALTH CREATORS

Many inheritors do not feel the need to become wealth creators, being quite content to live off the wealth earned by their predecessors. But this is not the case for all inheritors. There are dozens of examples of second, third, and later generation business personalities driving growth in their respective businesses like people possessed. They exude the hunger and ambition that drives people to strive to achieve ever higher levels of excellence in whatever they are doing. In this, the driving force behind a Mukesh Ambani or a Kumar Mangalam Birla is no different from the drive that a Virat Kohli or a Novak Djokovic feels when they take the field.

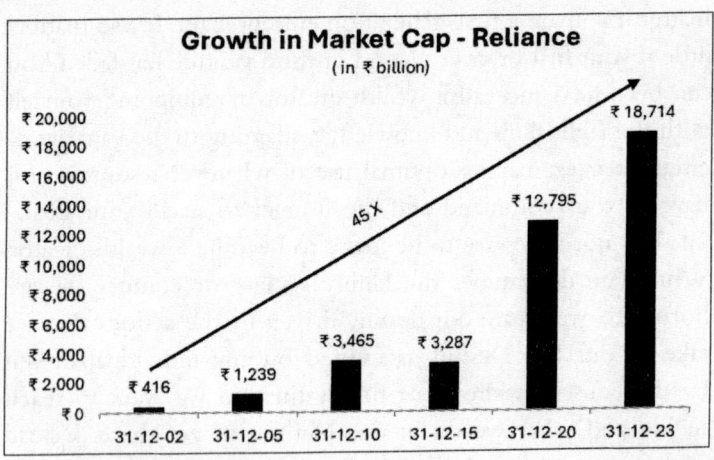

Image 1: Growth in market capital of Reliance from 2002 to 2023

Though Ambani and Birla benefitted from being born into established families, they had to prove themselves in the marketplace, sometimes in the face of scepticism over whether they fill the gargantuan shoes left behind by their respective legendary fathers. Though their famous surnames gave them a head start, it is their own achievements and track record as entrepreneurs and risk takers that have earned them the respect and admiration of their peers as well as the man on the street.

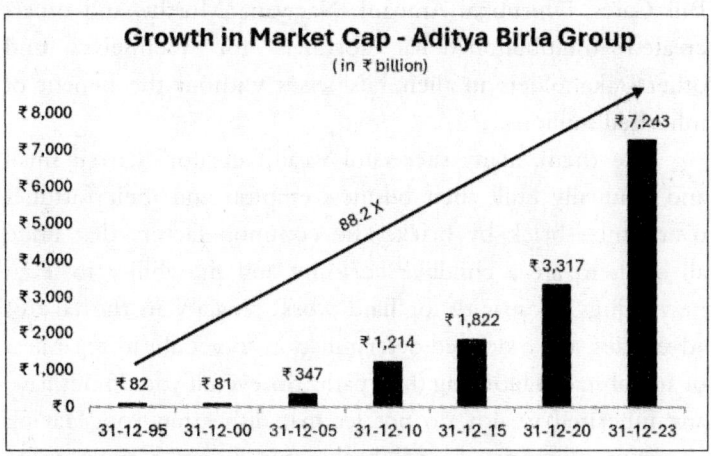

Image 2: Growth in market capital of Aditya Birla Group from 1995 to 2023

Like them, many other inheritors are actively involved in running and expanding their businesses within the country and across the world. They are intricately involved in the minutiae of all important decisions that impact their businesses and millions of people track their every move for indications on which way the economic winds are blowing. This shows that while a second or third generation businessperson may have an initial advantage over others, he/she must prove his/her mettle and use their privilege as a launchpad to expand the pool of wealth for all stakeholders—with prescience, diligence, hard work, and honesty of purpose. This is what differentiates a passive inheritor from the one who makes the transition to a wealth creator.

YOU DO NOT HAVE TO BE WEALTHY TO CREATE WEALTH

In the passage above, we have discussed how the likes of Bill Gates, Dhirubhai Ambani, Narayana Murthy, and others created multibillion-dollar fortunes for themselves and other stakeholders in their businesses without the benefit of inherited millions.

Like them, many successful wealth creators started small and gradually built their business empires and their fortunes over time—brick by brick. The common factors that unite all of them are a childlike curiosity and the ability to learn new things, a capacity for hard work, tenacity in the face of adversities, and a dogged determination to get ahead regardless of any obstacles blocking their paths. So, even if you do not have any inherited wealth, do not let that dishearten you. Having a corpus of money to fall back upon is not a prerequisite to becoming a wealth creator. Many of the world's biggest wealth creators started with nothing. What is essential is that you have a bankable idea, a feasible plan to monetize that idea, the hunger to execute that plan, and a stomach for risks. Wealth creation is not for the faint-hearted. But if you have all these attributes, there is no reason why you cannot become a successful wealth creator.

THE SECRET FORMULA

Unfortunately, there is no fixed formula for getting rich. What works for Person A may not work for Person B. The circumstances that Dhirubhai Ambani had to face could be quite different from the ones you will encounter in your journey as a wealth creator. So, you can, at best, use the examples of successful wealth creators as general guides for your journey but not as the definitive map that leads you to your desired destination.

However, while the circumstances of each wealth creator are unique, there is a certain set of imperatives that are common to all. These can be compared with the universal laws of nature which keep the cosmos in balance. These are very similar to the cause–effect relationship that is the foundation of everything that occurs. Together they create the secret sauce for wealth creation which can be picked up by one and all to become a wealth creator. We are calling them Laws of Wealth Creation which we shall learn in the following chapters. Learn and practise these, and you can be a wealth creator too.

Chapter 4

ADDING VALUE BY SOLVING A PROBLEM

Every business solves some problem for which society is willing to pay a price. Monetization of the solution to a problem leads to wealth creation.

Since time immemorial, the following piece of wisdom has been passed on from one generation to the next: if you help someone make money, you make money. This is nothing but adding value by solving a problem in the modern business world. Every business solves a problem for which society is willing to pay a price. Monetization of the solution to a problem leads to wealth creation.

Every product or service that we use addresses some need of ours—whether it is an agrarian product, an industrial product, or a service like transportation, healthcare, education, legal advice, etc. Even governments collect taxes in lieu of providing governance which is simply another term for being able to anticipate and fix problems that arise. Therefore, nations, too, are able to create wealth as a by-product of good governance.

How you help others, or how you or anyone else solves a problem varies widely depending on the specific situation, but all of them will help somebody become more productive, perform better, help someone get something and/or become a better and improved version of themselves.

The online Cambridge dictionary defines value addition as 'an improvement or addition to something that makes it worth more'. From this, it will be evident that adding value is the process of improving the usefulness, effectiveness, convenience, desirability, and attractiveness of an individual, product, or service. These usually go far beyond the immediate transactional needs of the moment and solve longer term problems faced by individuals, societies, or countries. Solving these problems allows an individual or a business earn money, thus, kick-starting the process of wealth creation.

Let us start with the most common, everyday examples of adding value by solving problems. Many people employ house helps such as cooks and drivers, use the services of plumbers, carpenters, painters, gardeners, and other similar service providers.

All of them help solve a specific problem—and they create value in the process of doing that. They are fulfilling a need of the society for specific services that allows the buyer of these services the freedom to engage in other productive activities.

For example, a householder—whether male or female, young, middle-aged or old—frees up their time to engage in monetizable work when he/she hires domestic help. The time he/she would have spent on cooking, ironing, cleaning, or driving can then be spent working on a project that earns monetary returns or engaging in leisure activities that rejuvenate the mind for the workdays that will follow.

The problem your domestic help solves for you is one of time management. And in doing so, he/she builds wealth—the difference is the threshold of wealth. Without much education or training, they are able to monetize the service that they provide. In some affluent families where domestic staff has been employed for generations, they get access to quality education, the ability to buy homes, and even fund medical emergencies.

By taking care of your regular chores, your domestic help gives you the time and the freedom to engage in more productive labour, the output from which adds value to your own life and creates wealth for your and, by extension, for the society you are a part of. Man has been striving to add value for himself and his society since the dawn of time. It is a fundamental concept of life and has been the basic building block of all progress and wealth creation down the ages. Value addition is a multi-faceted concept without which wealth creation, and indeed, social and material progress, would not be possible.

MULTIFACETED MEANING OF VALUE ADDITION

History is full of examples of intrepid men and women thinking out of the box, solving problems for society, or empires, or even themselves, and creating mountains of wealth for all stakeholders involved in the process.

It was Christopher Columbus's quest to find a sea route to India that led to the European 'discovery' of the New World that we now know as America. That was an era when empires expanded by conquering and annexing new territories to their domains. So, finding new territories with which to expand their empires added value for these European nations. The wealth extracted from the conquered territories added to the wealth of the conquering empires. Columbus and other voyagers like him helped find new lands and new sources of revenue—in this case, men and material from the New World—that created untold wealth for societies in Europe, albeit at the cost of great suffering to the native cultures in America and the rest of the world.

Throughout history, empires have been driven by expansion. The need for expansion was driven by an empire's need to sustain its sovereignty—by maintaining a strong military to protect itself. This required resources to train and pay the best military leaders, mercenaries, men, animals, and materials. An invincible empire had to be ever expanding.

The search for ever newer sources of wealth led to the 'discoveries' of new lands, not only in the two Americas but also elsewhere in the world. The intrepid adventurers who led these missions were solving a critical problem—the need for new resources. In doing so, they were adding to their own wealth and that of their governments and societies.

Likewise, great philosophers and thinkers like Chanakya, a political strategist who is known as the author of *Arthashastra*, one of the world's greatest and earliest texts on statecraft, politics, and economics, also added massive value to his society and history. By strategizing the ascent of an ambitious young man, Chandragupta Maurya, to the throne of Magadha and then by advising him on governance, diplomacy, and kingship, he helped usher in the first large empire in recorded Indian history and heralded a centuries-long period of peace, prosperity, and progress in the country. By helping to establish a centralized temporal authority across most of the length and breadth of his vast country, he solved the problem of political disunity within India where small kingdoms were frequently fighting among themselves. He helped lay the foundation of an empire that was larger, more populous, and richer than the Roman empire and, thus, set the conditions for wealth creation throughout the realm for several generations.

Sir Alexander Fleming's discovery of the world's first antibiotic in 1928, which he called penicillin, has been dubbed the single greatest victory mankind has ever achieved over disease. In the century since that discovery, penicillin has lived up to that billing by saving millions of people, thus enabling them to survive ailments that could have proved fatal in earlier times. By helping prolong lives, Sir Alexander solved a critical problem—of many people dying in their prime when they still had lots to contribute. This allowed many of them to carry on creating wealth for themselves and their countries and, thus, contributed in no small measure to wealth creation for society at large.

From the earliest times, man has dreamt of flying. Ancient civilizations like India and Greece have stories of humans trying to fly. The story of Pushpak Vimana and other flying craft are well known to most people familiar with Indian mythology. In Greek mythology, there is the story of Icarus, who dreamt of flying like a bird but met with a tragic end. The dream of flying remained just that—a dream—till two American brothers, Orville and Wilbur Wright demonstrated that it was indeed possible for humans to fly. Their invention solved a crucial problem for the modern world—of a fast and reliable means of transporting men and material between the furthest corners of the world.

There are thousands of other examples of scientists, innovators, adventurers, explorers, thinkers, and philosophers such as Thomas Alva Edison, Albert Einstein, Sir Isaac Newton, Ferdinand Magellan, Aristotle, Socrates, among others, who helped create a great deal of wealth not just for themselves but also for their stakeholders by adding substantial value to them.

BUSINESSES AND VALUE ADDITION

Businesses have traditionally been at the centre of wealth creation in society. Adding value and creating wealth is the raison d'etre of a business. When businesses offer a solution to a problem, customers are willing to pay for it. That is the equation that leads to wealth creation.

There is, therefore, a direct relationship between a successful enterprise and wealth creation. They do this by remaining ahead of the curve for adding value to their customers by constantly pursuing innovation, research and development, and reinvention. As a result of doing this, they become a source for job creation and therefore wealth creation for society.

Look around and you will see that every business offers a solution to a problem being faced by customers. Take the example of Apple. Its iconic founder Steve Jobs once famously said: 'Some people say, "Give the customers what they want." But that's not my approach. Our job is to figure out what they're going to want before they do. I think Henry Ford once said, "If I'd asked customers what they wanted, they would have told me, A faster horse!" People don't know what they want until you show it to them. That's why I never rely on market research. Our task is to read things that are not yet on the page.'

Today, that one device in the pocket of a customer helps solve dozens of problems. When was the last time you saw a mobile phone advertisement that extolled its voice quality or connectivity? Mobile phones now track people's health parameters, fitness statistics, do their calculations, help people navigate their way to unfamiliar destinations, make notes, store data, stream music, movies and games, take and store photographs and do a lot more. It is at once your bank, a payment interface, a restaurant order service, a social media gateway, a scanner, camera, and music player.

A mobile phone, thus, solves myriad problems for users and helps add value and, thus, creates wealth—for all stakeholders, such as the phone manufacturer, the users, and the app developers. By giving people easy access to technology, these devices have democratized the digital world, and this has helped add billions of dollars of wealth to the global economy. It is no wonder Apple is counted amongst the most valuable businesses of our times with cash reserves of $162 billion, which is more than the GDP of many countries.

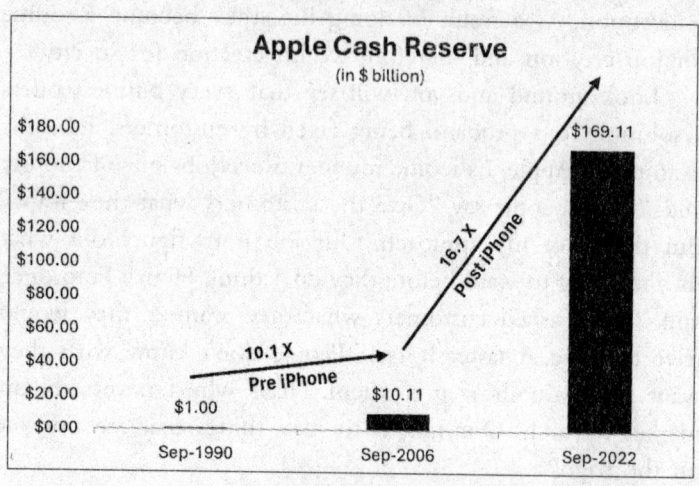

Image 3: Apple's cash reserves before the launch of the iPhone and after

In the field of transportation, people progressed from walking and then travelling on horseback and bullock carts to faster modes of transport when the progress of science helped develop the steam engine and the motor car. With the invention of aircraft, especially jet engines, during World War II, travel that earlier took months and even years could now be completed in a matter of hours. Given the interconnected nature of businesses and the economy, one will be hard put to find anyone whose personal fortunes had not been impacted in one way or the other by the improvement in transport technology and infrastructure. By bringing physical connectivity within the reach of almost everyone on earth, airline companies, aircraft makers, and their associate companies have helped add billions of dollars of value to society and generated wealth for themselves and every sector of the economy.

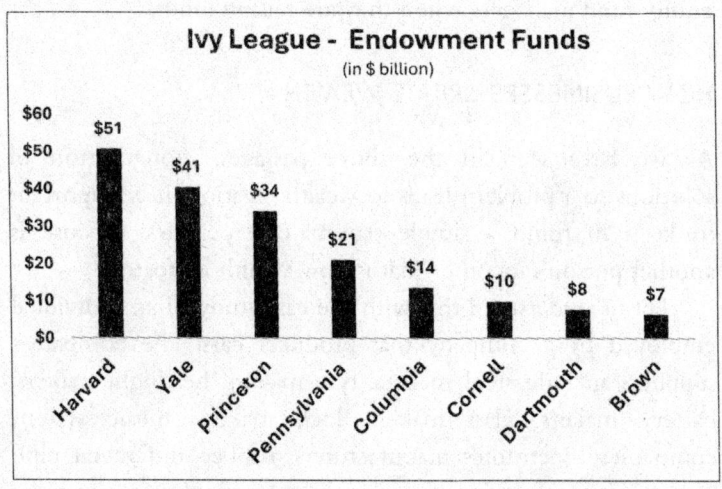

Image 4: Ivy League colleges have accumulated large endowment funds

It is the same with businesses in the health and education sectors. Good quality education and healthcare was once the preserve of the privileged, but the efforts of entrepreneurs in these fields have democratized access. By solving the problems of health and education, they have added incalculable value to society and helped create wealth for society and for themselves. Consider the examples of Ivy League institutions such as Harvard, Yale, or Columbia University. Not only do they add value and help society create wealth by imparting quality education to students from hundreds of countries, they also have accumulated their very own large endowment funds running into billions of dollars. Harvard tops this list with US$ 50.9 billion at the end of September 2022 followed by Yale at US$ 41.4 billion and Stanford at US$ 36.3 billion. The large investible reserves that they sit on make them sought after institutional investors for venture capital and private equity fund managers when they are raising funds.

HOW BUSINESSES CREATE WEALTH

As we have seen in the above passages, monetization of solutions to a problem leads to wealth creation. It is important to keep in mind a simple truism: one person's expense is another person's income. That is how wealth is created.

Let us understand this with the case study of an individual employed by a company that produces cars. The company's suppliers include steel makers, tyre makers, headlight makers, battery makers, glass makers, lock makers, music system companies, electronics manufacturers, rubber and metal pipe companies, leather factories, and dozens of others.

All of these companies, in turn, buy inputs and components from their suppliers. This creates a huge ecosystem that is self-sustaining, which grows over time, bringing more and more people under its ambit.

Now, let us come back to the example of the salaried person we mentioned earlier. This individual uses the salary he/she earns to pay for food, clothing, shelter, transport, education, healthcare, leisure, for himself/herself and all dependents, and also puts away a set amount every month as savings. This creates another ecosystem of wealth creation, where each recipient of money from this individual spends it for his/her own set of expenses. This again generates revenues, profits, and savings downstream. This process continues in a self-sustaining virtuous cycle and creates wealth and prosperity by solving problems faced by individuals in society.

VALUE ADDITION AND WEALTH CREATION BEYOND BUSINESS

Though businesses are generally accepted as the primary vehicle for value addition and wealth creation, there are lots of other institutions that add value for both individuals and society and create wealth for everyone.

Let us begin with the family, which is the basic unit of society. It is from one's family that an individual first learns core values and from which a person acquires his/her basic character. It will be fair to say that every individual's personality is shaped in large measure by his/her family background and its socio-cultural moorings.

The value system that a person imbibes in his/her formative years become the frame around which the rest of that individual's character is formed. This has a major impact on the value he creates for society through his life.

The next value creating institution a person encounters in life is school. A good basic education is the foundation on which the rest of an individual's life stands. So, good educational institutions—schools, colleges, and institutions of higher learning—play a very important role in adding value to society. They solve the problem of illiteracy, ignorance, and the lack of scientific enquiry. By democratizing the spread of knowledge and by inculcating a scientific temper in students, these institutions help in the process of wealth creation by equipping society with the wherewithal to deal with the problems it confronts.

Contrary to popular misconception, governments can also be wealth creators. Governments add value to society by delivering good governance. This includes clean, corruption-free administration, establishment of the rule of law, provision for good quality civic amenities, functioning grievance redressal mechanisms, and an enabling atmosphere for economic, social, cultural, and political development. Each one of these addresses a key problem of society and solving them creates a fertile ground for individuals and institutions to create wealth for themselves, their societies, and their country. Countries that rank high on these parameters are also the ones with high standards of living, high per capita GDP, and good social indicators.

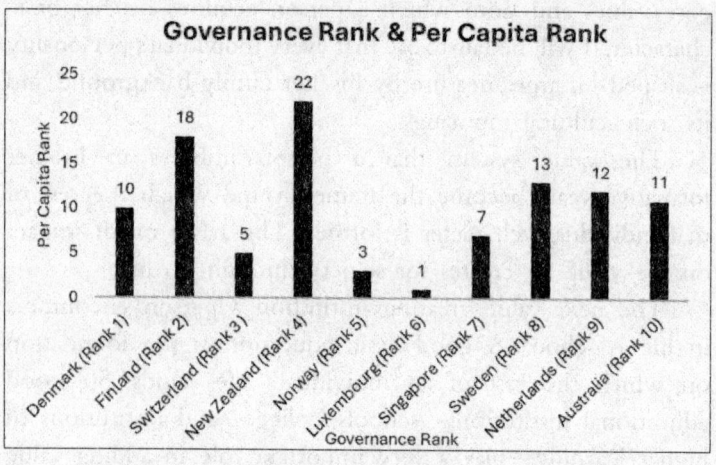

Image 5: Countries with high governance ranks are also the ones with high per capita GDP

Good governance also rewards those who deliver it. Arvind Panagariya, former vice chairman of NITI Aayog, said: 'CMs who deliver growth levels higher than their predecessor have been returned to power in the last 25 years.[*] They include (with their tenures and growth rates delivered in the years preceding the last election won): Narendra Modi, Gujarat, 2001–14: 10.2%; Shivraj Singh Chauhan, MP, 2003–18: 7.2%; Naveen Patnaik, Odisha, 2000–till date: 6.3%.

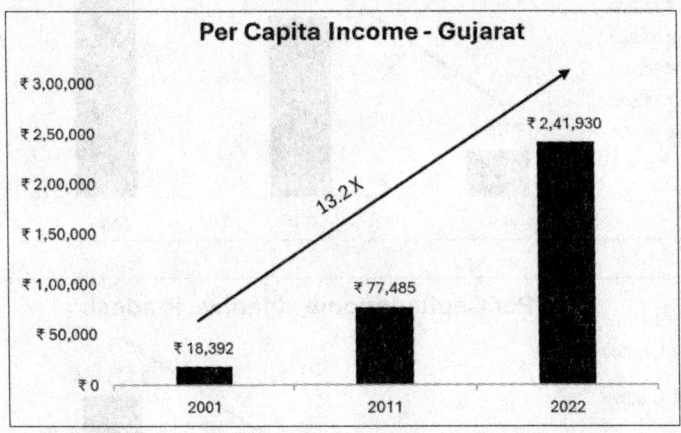

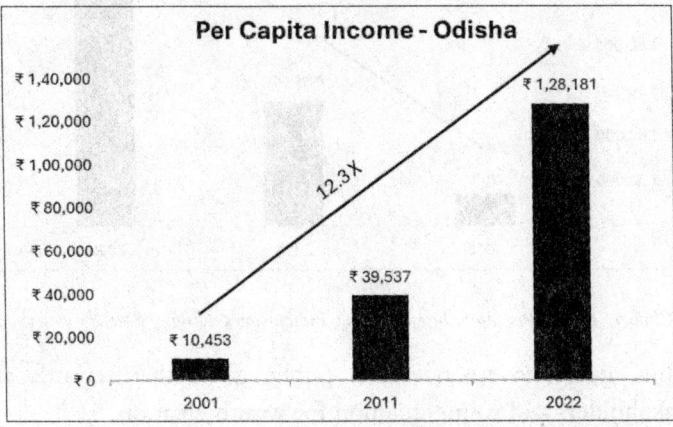

---

[*]'Caste census is a wrong number', Arvind Panagariya, *Times of India*, 19 October 2023.

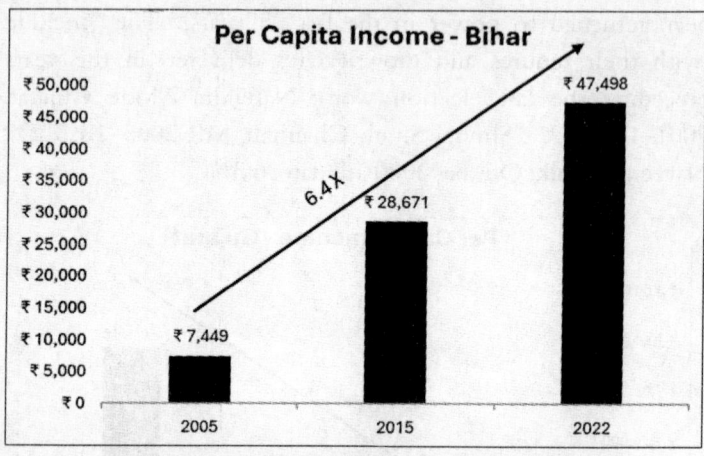

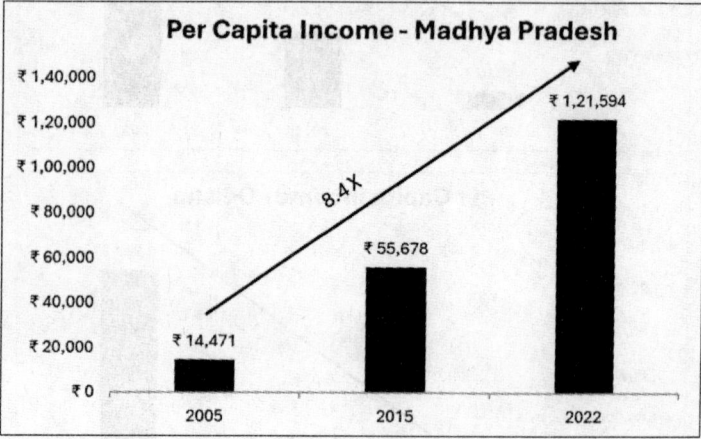

Images 6 to 9: Per capita income of four Indian states marking a steady growth

Thus, good governance is a public good that rewards all stakeholders and is sine qua non for wealth creation.

Likewise, non-government organizations (NGOs) also create wealth by solving problems faced by society. Here, the profits are used not for personal benefit but for the good of society as a whole. For example, NGOs working for the education of girls from the underprivileged sections of the society not only uplift women but also lift entire families out of poverty. An educated girl will be healthier, get married later than usual, plan a smaller family, and would most likely earn an income. This would lead to economic development by an increase in the productivity of society in terms of per capita income in two ways—a fall in the fertility rate and increased participation of women in the labour force. There is, thus, a key difference between businesses that create wealth for themselves and NGOs that work strictly on a not-for-profit basis.

Chapter 5

HUNGER VERSUS GREED

Hunger is the pursuit of growth with wealth creation as its by-product. It is a positive attribute driven by the larger goal of lifting the entire ecosystem.

Greed is the pursuit of wealth itself which often leads to its unequal distribution.

The seed for wealth creation is the aspiration to have it. You cannot be a wealth creator unless you believe in having wealth. This is manifested in two kinds of organizations that we see in the world—for profit and not for profit—each has a very different motive for existence.

The former is driven by the hunger for personal wealth creation, while the latter is driven by the desire to give back to society. Therefore, members of for-profit organizations may create personal wealth whereas those working in not-for-profit organizations create wealth not for themselves but for the society at large.

However, there is a very fine line between hunger and greed. While both could lead to wealth creation, the means adopted in each case would be very different. In the case of hunger, wealth is a means to an end, while in the case of greed, wealth is the end itself. Hunger can lead to emancipation of society while greed often leads to inequal distribution of wealth in society. Though both lead to wealth creation, hunger is a more long-lasting fuel compared to greed.

DEFINING HUNGER

In the Hindu tradition, Lakshmi, the goddess of wealth, blesses those who crave her presence and stays with those who value and respect her. That is where we see the fundamental distinction between the two types of organizations that create wealth—those driven by the profit motive, and those that are fuelled by their not-for-profit aspirations.

In the context of this chapter, hunger can be defined as the aspiration for creating one's desired destiny in life. It begins with setting goals and then making intense effort to get there. During the hunter/gatherer era of prehistoric times, hunger was only for food and the effort expended was to find nourishment. During the agrarian period, as humans learnt the science and art of cultivation, the meaning of hunger evolved to increased ownership of land as the source of wealth. If one could have more land, one could produce more, sell more, and create more wealth. The Industrial Revolution of the eighteenth century unleased the hidden knowledge behind science—hunger then involved setting up mechanized production facilities to produce more and more goods at lower costs, sell more than anyone else, and create more wealth. In the current era of the Technological Revolution, hunger could mean creating new-age businesses driven by innovation, which could access consumers anywhere anytime, thus, making it possible to sell more products and services to more and more customers unrestricted by limitations of geography and time. Hunger then is nothing but the pursuit of growth with wealth creation as its by-product. It is a positive attribute driven by the larger goal of lifting the entire ecosystem.

IMPORTANCE OF HUNGER IN WEALTH CREATION

We have discussed in the previous chapter how adventurers like Christopher Columbus, entrepreneurs like Steve Jobs, and thinkers like Chanakya laid the foundations of great empires that went on to create great wealth for their respective societies and massive fortunes for many individuals. The common thread running through all their actions, separated as they were by several centuries, many continents, and thousands of miles, was one trait: hunger!

If wealth is the effect, then hunger is its cause. If wealth is the visible form of energy, then hunger is its seed. The journey of wealth creation cannot begin without sowing the seeds of hunger. And hunger is nothing but a growth-oriented mindset. It constantly engages the human mind on how to get to the next level. It could be scaling up of a business, improving one's skill set, scientific enquiry leading to innovation, and even the pursuit of the meaning of life. A growth-oriented mindset sets us on the path of growth and wealth is a by-product of growth in any form. We see it all around us. Can there be a flowering or fruition if the plant refuses to grow? Can there be food if the crop does not grow? Flowers, fruits, and food are nature's bounties and a form of wealth that gets created as a by-product of growth.

Hunger is that dynamic force that energizes a person to embark on the pursuit of wealth. It drives people to think well beyond the scope of satisfying their immediate needs and manifests itself by relentlessly driving individuals to achieve their goal of financial success and economic well-being.

DIFFERENCE BETWEEN HUNGER AND GREED

Calling someone money-minded is seen as a negative attribute. Being money-minded is seen as being less than honourable and most people would take offence at being so labelled. If wealth creation is such a desirable and cherished goal, why is being money-minded considered bad?

Wealth creation and money-mindedness are, indeed, rather different, although at first glance they appear so similar as to be almost identical. The former is driven by hunger and the latter by greed. Many people cannot distinguish between these two and equate one with the other. If hunger is misunderstood as greed, it will be regressive for society as people will keep away from wealth creation—any largescale move away from wealth creation in society will impoverish everyone.

Definitionally, both hunger and greed can lead to wealth creation, at least in the short term, but then their paths begin to diverge.

In case of hunger wealth is always a means to an end and never the end goal. Wealth is merely the logical by-product of hunger, of pursuing a dream. Whereas in the case of greed, wealth becomes the end goal. Let's take the example of two doctors—one is driven by the goal of healing his patients and the other is driven by how much can he earn from his patients. Both are qualified professionals but their approach towards wealth creation is different. One is driven by doing good to the society and the second one is driven by a short-term opportunistic approach. Both will create wealth in the short term. However, the first doctor is more likely to earn the trust of his community and build credibility, which will pull more and more people to him and help him create more wealth over a longer period of time whereas the opposite may happen with the second doctor.

Let us take the case of two well-known families from the financial services sector to further elucidate the above point. The Rothschilds are a highly respected and incredibly wealthy family that have endured for more than two centuries at the high table of global finance. The name inspires trust and admiration, and this has allowed the family to prosper and grow over several generations and across almost every continent in the world. The Rothschild family has managed to pass down the hunger for growth from generation to generation and this has allowed them to continue generating wealth for themselves and their stakeholders.

At the other end of the spectrum is the example of Bernie Madoff and his short-lived financial services empire. Though it reached dizzying heights at its peak, it proved to be a house of cards and collapsed when it came to light that much of their fabled wealth existed only on paper and that the Madoff empire was partly the result of an elaborate Ponzi scheme. This is a classic example of greed generating very high short-term gains but then reducing everything to dust.

For almost three decades from the late 1980s, Bill Gates was ranked the richest man in the world. His stake in Microsoft was (and remains) the source of his wealth. It was his hunger for success and greater glory that pushed him to set a punishing schedule for himself and his team to keep producing, updating, and upgrading software that powered more than 80 per cent of the world's personal computers.

When he finally called it a day at Microsoft, a company he had founded in his parents' garage, he decided to give away most of his humungous fortune to the underprivileged across the world, including in India. The Bill and Melinda Gates Foundation is the world's largest privately funded NGO and is doing commendable work in a number of critical sectors and helping governments around the world fight poverty, disease, inequity, and climate change.

As this example and that of many others such as the Rockefeller Foundation, the Tata Trusts, Reliance Foundation, Shiv Nadar Foundation, Azim Premji Foundation, etc., will show, the great hunger exhibited by the founders of the businesses that funded these charities ultimately led to a large chunk of their wealth being channelled for the purpose of social emancipation and the greatest common good.

Since wealth is not the end goal of hunger it gets transmitted across society, thus lifting everyone in the ecosystem, making the 'Wealth Effect' evident. In case of greed, on the other hand, since wealth becomes the end in itself, it gets hoarded. Greed, therefore, becomes the barrier to the transmission of wealth across society, leading to greater inequality between the haves and the have nots, which could eventually result in social strife.

So, if one considers motivation, means, and outcomes, hunger can, in the light of the foregoing discussion, be considered a positive and aspirational impulse. It often results in personal improvement and social upliftment following large and small acts of philanthropy.

An entrepreneur driven by hunger to create wealth is usually perceived to be more ethical in his/her approach to business. These entrepreneurs and the organizations they lead are often seen as good corporate citizens who work hard, innovate, and deliver results with honesty and sincerity.

Businesses driven by hunger create wealth for all stakeholders—customers, employees, vendors, partners, and shareholders. They follow good governance practices, build trust in the society, and become a benchmark for ethical living. Infosys is a good example of this and has inspired a generation of entrepreneurs in India. On the contrary, in the case of businesses driven by greed, the intent is to maximize the profits for the shareholders at the expense of all other stakeholders. They may be ever willing to compromise their ethics and governance standards and end up becoming a source of trust deficit in society.

On the same parameters of motivation, means, and outcomes, greed emerges as less desirable. Being driven by greed is selfish as it lacks a motivation beyond personal gratification and there is no social purpose involved in the process.

As mentioned above, greed can result in social tensions, rising inequality, and a breakdown in society's moral compass. It usually leads to a situation where a few people benefit to the detriment of the majority and often does not create lasting prosperity.

Therefore, the pursuit of wealth should be balanced with ethical considerations, integrity, and responsibility.

HUNGER VERSUS GREED

Entrepreneurs driven by hunger are usually better placed to deliver long-term growth in a sustainable manner than those fuelled by greed as the latter are usually more opportunistic and less motivated by the possibility of beneficial outcomes in the distant future.

Because of this, people and businesses driven by hunger are usually able to win the trust of their employees, customers, suppliers, and society.

Take the example of any business that has lasted beyond a threshold of twenty-five years. You will find that all of them, almost without exception, were led by people driven by hunger.

Now, consider some of the biggest scams of the past three decades—the Harshad Mehta stock market scam of 1992, the Ketan Parekh scam of 2001, the Bernie Madoff scam of 2008, or the Satyam scam of 2009. All these individuals were driven by greed and were feted as great wealth creators by the public as well as the authorities before this came to be known. Two of them—Madoff and B. Ramalinga Raju of Satyam—held public positions, the former as chairman of Nasdaq and the latter as chairman of a publicly listed company that was at the time India's fourth-largest software exporter.

All of them were seen as great wealth creators and, indeed, all of them had become the darlings of investors as they delivered very high returns on investments. But away from the public gaze, their greed had got the better of their ethics and their business sense. All of them were authors of large schemes that seemed glitzy and successful at first glance, but turned out to be scams. The old adage—if something looks too good to be true, it probably is—turned out to be true.

Despite the large amounts of short-term wealth these shooting stars of the business world had created for themselves and their investors, it was all destroyed in a flash when their scams came to light. In all these cases, thousands of people lost their life savings, there was a general loss of trust among common people and even respected business leaders began to be looked at with suspicion. The misdeeds of a few greedy men cast a long shadow over the entire financial systems of India and the US, and it took many years and lots of hard work on the parts of many wise heads to restore public trust in the systems that form the backbone of the financial world.

Now, contrast this with business houses such as N. M. Rothschild & Co., Tata Sons, Aditya Birla Group, Mahindra & Mahindra, Unilever, and others. These multi-generational businesses have been led by people hungry for building an institution and this has enabled them to become respected household names not only in their domestic markets but also in large parts of the world outside India.

Not only do the leaders of these business houses create wealth for themselves and their families but also for the ecosystem of stakeholders in dozens of countries around the world, thus, helping perpetuate the virtuous cycle of prosperity.

It will be clear from the above, therefore, that although greed may give great short-term returns, hunger is a better fuel for long-term wealth creation, sustainable growth, and widespread prosperity.

INDIVIDUAL HUNGER VERSUS STATE CAPITALISM

Even if we accept that hunger is more desirable than greed—and not many people will disagree with that—there are still some who claim that any sort of wealth creation somehow militates against the idea of equity, egalitarianism, and equality. They turn the axiom 'one person's expense is another person's income' on its head by arguing that by the same logic, one person's gain is another person's loss and add that in the real world, markets are manipulated to ensure the rich get richer and the poor get poorer. Market-oriented economies, by their very nature, cannot deliver equity to all their citizens, they argue, pointing to the now defunct socialist societies to prove their point. These countries, they add, were run according to socialist principles that precluded any need for wealth creation, either by hunger or greed. So, these not-for-profit societies were morally superior and more egalitarian than their counterparts in the market economies.

Some people may find this reasoning ideologically satisfying but it is factually incorrect. It is now common knowledge that the countries of East Europe that followed a socialist economic model collapsed under the weight of their economic inefficiencies though they did manage to do well on most social indicators.

For easy comparison, let us take the examples of West Germany and East Germany from Europe and North Korea and South Korea from Asia. These countries were formed following the partition of Germany in the aftermath of World War II and the division of Korea following the Korean War.

West Germany chose to continue as a market economy but its eastern part, which came under the influence of the Soviet Union began its tryst with socialism after the war was over. Likewise, at the end of the Korean War in 1953, North Korea embarked on the path of socialist development while South Korea blundered about for a few years before adopting the capitalist model of economic development.

West Germany soon established itself as the powerhouse economy of Europe. Not much was known about the actual state of affairs in East Germany as it was behind the Iron Curtain. Within a few years, however, it became apparent that socialism had not been able to deliver the desired results for East Germany and that the western part of the country, fuelled by the hunger of its citizens and the power of the market, had surged ahead. A steady stream of people began to trickle out of socialist East Germany into West Germany. By 1989, when the two parts reunited, West Germany was far ahead of the East in every economic and most social indicators.

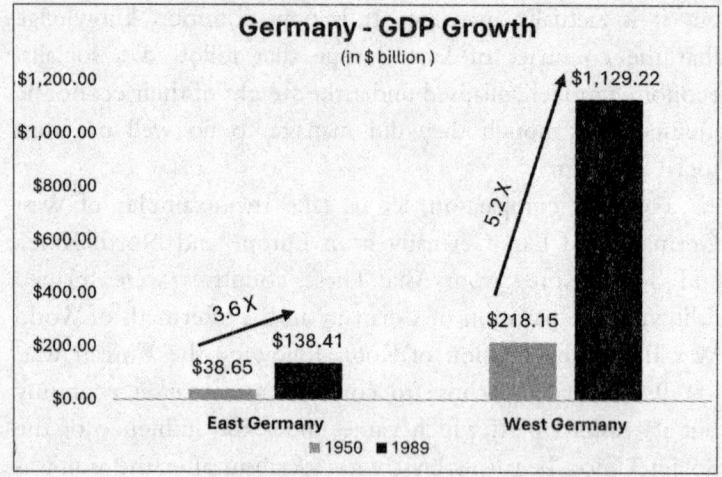

Image 10: The growth in the GDP of West Germany was far ahead of East Germany

The economic trajectories of North Korea and South Korea have followed a similar pattern. Today, South Korea, which was considered the more backward of the two halves in 1953, is considered a First World nation with a GDP of US$1.7 trillion and a per capita income of US$33,147 (both figures for 2023). North Korea, on the other hand, is pariah state and an economic failure with a GDP of $48.3 billion and a per capita income of US$1,116 (both figures for 2022). Incidentally, South Korea's largest business house Samsung's annual turnover is US$200 billion or four times the GDP of North Korea!

Closer home, consider the example of India. Before 1991, official policy looked disdainfully at wealth creation and discouraged the profit motive and dubbed it greed. As a result the Indian economy was marked by shortages of almost every item, rampant black marketing, shoddy goods, and widespread poverty. The country was on the brink of bankruptcy and had to mortgage its gold reserves to the Bank of England to access a loan to stave off a payments default. After 1991, when economic reforms legitimized the profit motive and recognized hunger as a desirable fuel for growth, India slowly shed its image of a poor Third World nation and has slowly emerged as a viable and attractive wealth generator for investors all over the world. The path of encouraging hunger-fuelled economic development has led to this transformation. According to the latest UN report on Multidimensional Poverty Index, around 415 million people, or about a third of all Indians, exited poverty in the fifteen years from 2005-2021. Ironically, it was the much-derided profit motive, rather than nominally pro-poor rhetoric, that ultimately helped India's poor.[*]

Here too, we see that a hunger for wealth creation delivers far better results and helps everyone—rich, middle class, and poor—improve their standard of living. It helps to spread affluence across society. That is because distribution of wealth has to be preceded by wealth creation. If you keep cutting chunks from the existing pie of wealth, you will soon be left with nothing to distribute—unless you find some way of growing the pie constantly even as you keep carving out pieces to provide for everyone. That was the fundamental flaw in societies and countries that posited themselves as alternatives to the wealth creation model followed by market-led economies like the US, EU, Japan, South Korea, and ASEAN. Finally, it was the weakness of their economic model and its inability to create wealth that let them down and caused the Soviet Bloc to collapse

---

[*]PEW Report

Therefore, it will be fair to say that not only is hunger superior to greed in the context of wealth creation, but it is also far more effective than any system that artificially suppresses that hunger and supplants it with a utopian ideology.

Chapter 6

INPUT VERSUS OUTPUT

The cause-and-effect equation applies in every field. Desired outcomes, or outputs, require inputs. The Law of Karma is at work—in life and in wealth creation.

There is a cause-and-effect relationship in everything around us. Wealth, too, is a by-product of effort. In our pursuit of wealth, we remain invariably fixated on wealth, the end, which is the output, rather than on the means that lead to that end, or what we need to do to create it—in other words, the input.

A farmer has to prepare his land at the beginning of the season to harvest a good crop. An investor has to invest to get returns. A business has to invest in order to expand and grow. We have to first give in order to receive. Rather than chasing the output, we have to remain focused on input. Desired outcomes—or output—follow from required inputs. It is the law of karma which is at work—in life and in wealth creation.

THE CAUSE-AND-EFFECT RELATIONSHIP

Hollywood movie mogul Samuel Goldwyn famously said: 'The harder I work the luckier I get.' This inspirational quote has become popular among corporate executives and at B-schools around the world. At its core, it is an honest acknowledgement of the cause-and-effect relationship between hard work or effort or input and success or reward or output.

This is something we are taught from childhood—that people make their own future based on their actions.

The simplest example of this is the act of flicking on a switch to light a lamp. In case of an individual working in an organization, performing as per expectations or beyond helps him/her earn the trust of his immediate stakeholders—peers, colleagues, and seniors. This makes the employee stand out as someone who is dependable. The ecosystem can trust him/her for his/her ability and willingness to deliver on greater responsibilities which leads to role expansion. Promotion, increment, reward are by-products of the bigger role leading to wealth creation. On the other hand, poor performance can lead to career stagnation and, therefore, no wealth creation.

Let us take the example of X who wants to build an investment portfolio. If he/she does this on the basis of market rumours or 'hot tips' from friends and colleagues, the returns will depend entirely on luck. My practical, real-life experience shows that more often than not such investment decisions fail to deliver the desired results. On the other hand, if X invests time and effort on research and consults and seeks advice from experts, he/she increases the chances of getting good returns on his/her investment.

This same principle of cause and effect will be evident in the case of businesses. The goal of all businesses is to grow shareholder wealth. To achieve this, many businesses seek to expand into newer markets and launch new or upgraded products. If this is done without sufficient homework and with only a superficial understanding of the market, consumer preference, pricing, and macro-economic conditions, the chances of failure will be very high. On the other hand, if the management has invested in thorough planning and proper groundwork, it increases the chances of success quite significantly.

We see this same relationship between cause and effect in the start-up universe. The business papers are often full of reports on angel investors betting millions on start-up entrepreneurs based solely on the power of an idea. But contrary to popular misconception, these angel investors and venture capitalists are not basing their investment decisions solely on their hunch. Their investments are often backed by detailed research, which in this case, is the input. The returns of their investments, whenever it materializes, is the output.

From the above, it will be clear that in the context of wealth creation, the cause-and-effect relationship refers to the direct correlation between a set of actions or moves undertaken by an individual and the results of that effort. Thus, wealth creation should not be seen as a random act or a stroke of luck but as the end result of enduring effort and strategic actions in pursuit of a desired goal. It must be noted here that windfall profits and speculative gains are usually one-off events and cannot be considered a sustainable means of wealth creation. Achieving financial prosperity is always the end product of a long and laborious process of research, hard work, teamwork, planning, judicious risk taking, and relentless execution. These inputs are essential and the cause of the end product, or effect, which is the creation of wealth.

The real world is full of examples of this cause-and-effect relationship between input and output. No one has ever earned money in a vacuum. Pick up any business newspaper on any day of the week. You will almost certainly come across several news items on companies announcing plans to invest in capital expenditure. The scale might vary from a few crores in the case of early-stage start-ups to several thousand crores of rupees in the case of market leaders and industry behemoths. The goal of all these companies is the same: to grow their revenues, improve profitability, and grow shareholders' wealth. These, too, are examples of cause and effect. The input is the heavy dose of investment these companies are making while the output will be the enhanced profits these investments will yield in future.

This cause and effect relationship is seen not only in the case of businesses but also in various socio-economic investments. The government invests thousands of crores of rupees on building highways, airports, ports, irrigation canals, sanitation systems, and other social infrastructure like schools and hospitals. Besides providing income to businesses that are involved in their construction, these projects are also enablers and facilitators of the wealth creation efforts of citizens at large. They increase business opportunities for a host of entrepreneurs and companies and give returns to the government in the form of higher taxes from increased economic growth.

This relationship will also be in evidence in the allocation of public funds for education. By imparting education to wide swathes of people, the government is improving the productivity of the population which enables them to live better lives, earn more, save more, and create more wealth for themselves and for society as a whole.

THE MEANS TO AN END

Let us now examine how the principle of a cause–effect relationship helps in the wealth creation for an individual. This can be understood by the equation of investing:

$$FV = PV \star (1+R)^{\wedge} N$$

Where FV is the future value and PV the present value of the investment, while R and N are the rate of return and the time period of the investment.

The future value of your wealth or the effect or output is a function of the cause or the input which is the invested or the present value of your wealth that would grow at a given rate of return over a given period of time. Hence, it follows from this equation that wealth creation is the excess of future value over present value. In other words, wealth creation can be defined as the growth in wealth. The input is the investment that you make, and the output is the growth in wealth that results from that initial investment.

The equation is simple: unless you make the investment today, you will not get returns tomorrow. This is a basic law of investment. The other axiom of investment is the more you invest, given the same rate of return and time period of investment, the more wealth you are likely to create in the future.

Let us see how this works with real-life examples. Person A invests ₹1 lakh in a business for a 10 per cent share of the business. Person B investments ₹2 lakh for a 20 per cent share. Quite naturally, when dividends are disbursed at the end of the year, Person B will get double the share of profits that Person A receives.

What we learn from this classic equation of wealth creation is that for the same rate of return and time period of investment, the quantum of wealth creation is directly correlated with the quantum of investment.

Let us return to the example of the farmer we mentioned at the beginning of this chapter. This farmer buys the best quality seeds, ploughs his land diligently, sows the seeds, and waters and tends to his crops through the season. Another farmer who owns the neighbouring farm is very cost conscious; so, he buys seeds of a lower quality because they cost less; he also uses less water because that saves him expenses on running his diesel pump; and he also refuses to hire a tractor to plough his land. Instead, he follows the age-old method of using cattle for this purpose. All other things remaining constant and if the weather gods are generous, at the end of the season, the first farmer is more likely to get a bumper harvest, while the second farmer will be left aghast at the relatively poor quality of his yield. These examples prove the point above—that the amount one gets as returns depends on the amount one invests in the venture. The more one invests, the more one is likely to gain. The quality of investment also matters. A thoroughly researched and properly implemented plan is more likely to get rich returns than one that is superficially put together and shoddily executed.

This is how cause and effect, also called input and output, works in the realm of wealth creation.

INPUT OR OUTPUT

Most Indians will be familiar with the broad message of the Bhagavad Gita. One of its most famous shlokas in Chapter 2, Verse 47 says:

> *Karmanye vadhikaraste ma phaleshu kadachana*
> *Ma karmaphalaheturbhurma te sangostvakarmani*
>
> *You have the right to work but no rights to the fruits of your labour.*
> *Let not the fruits of action be your motive, nor let your attachment be to inaction.*

This ancient Indian wisdom is as true for spiritual upliftment as it is for other, more material aspects of life such as wealth creation. A crucial aspect of the cause-and-effect relationship in the creation of wealth is the focus on the means rather than on the desired end result. Many people lose track of this wisdom and become obsessed with their goal—to earn and accumulate more and more wealth. The process, thus, becomes less important than the outcome and this could lead, in many cases, to people straying from the path of integrity, which, as we have seen from the examples of people like Madoff, Harshad Mehta, Ketan Parekh, and others, can be a steep and slippery slope of the destruction of wealth both for self and for the ecosystem.

As we have discussed above, you have to invest in order to receive returns. The act of making that investment is the input. It is not possible to earn returns that are sustainable unless you make that initial investment and then back it up with diligent monitoring and follow-up.

From a practical perspective, too much focus on the end result can distract an individual from the task at hand, which is to ensure that the input is properly administered. Output, therefore, follows input. In the context of wealth creation, it can be understood that one should be focused only on input in order to create wealth.

We learnt in the previous chapter about the difference between hunger and greed when it comes to wealth creation. Can we connect the dots between the principle of hunger and greed and that of input and output in the context of wealth creation? The former is always focussed on the input and the latter on the output. It is the hunger for action, the hunger for enterprise, the hunger for achieving a larger purpose that creates wealth as a by-product. Bill Gates did not set out to become the world's richest person when he launched Microsoft; Steve Jobs could not have envisaged the kind of wealth he would create when he returned to Apple, a company he had founded and then been ousted from. Narayana Murthy and his co-founders at Infosys did not set for themselves the goal of becoming billionaires when they started their firm offering software coding services. All of them created unimaginable quantum of wealth in the process of doing something else very well.

On the other hand, greed and pursuit of output drives individuals to chase only the end goal at any cost. The motivation is self-enrichment rather than adding value for stakeholders that we discussed in Chapter 4. This approach could divert an individual from the path of ethical conduct to make compromises to realize his end goal of wealth creation. Moreover, wealth creation that is driven by greed and focussed only on the output could force an individual to assume risk which is beyond normal thus exposing him to the risk of erosion of wealth rather than creation. So, even from a practical point of view, it is always better to be driven by input and hunger rather than by output or greed.

Chapter 7

PURPOSE VERSUS NUMBERS

Businesses that are driven by their larger purpose become perpetual sources of wealth creation.

In an earlier chapter, we have seen that adding value by solving a problem leads to wealth creation. There is also a linear relationship between the number of people for whom you solve a problem and the amount of wealth that gets created. Most businesses are driven by this principle but sooner or later, they become commoditized. The pace of wealth creation could then slow down since the solution that the business offers is no longer unique.

However, if a business is driven by the larger purpose of having a positive impact on society, then that becomes an everlasting source of wealth creation. Such businesses are always ahead of the curve–adopting and often leading with best practices, know-how, and technology. Such businesses never go out of business and, therefore, remain a perennial source of wealth creation.

THE PURPOSE OF A BUSINESS

Every business is driven by the profit motive and is powered by the aspirations of its owners. This flows from the notion that the primary goal of the business is to earn money for its owners and provide sustenance to its stakeholders.

As we said at the beginning of this chapter, scale plays a very important role in wealth creation. The larger the number of people they solve problems for, the more a business is likely to earn. Thus, there are businesses that cater only to their local markets, there are those that serve customers across a larger area, like an entire state; then, there are businesses that are national in scale and ambition and, finally, there are large multinational corporations that sell their goods and services in several countries across the world.

Examples of local businesses include standalone restaurants, mom-and-pop retail stores, individual movie halls, and car servicing workshops. When these same businesses expand their operations and set up branches either by themselves or through franchisees beyond their place of origin in other parts of the state, they turn into businesses of the second type. HDFC Bank and Maruti Suzuki are examples of national businesses, while Microsoft, Volkswagen, Walt Disney & Co., and Citibank are truly international businesses with footprints straddling hundreds of countries across every continent in the world.

All these businesses are united by their goal of generating returns for their owners and shareholders and creating wealth for stakeholders in the process. But in recent years, the remit of businesses has expanded beyond merely generating financial returns. According to the latest thinking, businesses are also encouraged to focus on the social aspect of their activities by way of corporate social responsibility. At the same time, they are expected to pay attention to the environmental impact of their business while following ethical governance practices. This has led to the emergence of the ESG (Environmental, Social, and Governance) framework. Society now expects businesses to promote the well-being of the communities they work with.

There is also a strong school of thought that believes that even while focusing on maximizing profits and shareholder value, businesses should avoid short-term measures and concentrate on long-term value creation not only for its owners and shareholders but for all stakeholders such as customers, vendors, employees, and the community at large.

However, it is not mandatory for all businesses to be driven by a larger purpose or even by the goal of long-term value creation; but business history shows that companies that develop a social conscience and manage their affairs in alignment with broader societal objectives typically gain prestige, credibility, investor backing, and usually create value and wealth for all stakeholders over much longer time horizons than the ones that do not.

The BSE Sensex is a widely tracked index and is considered a proxy for the health of the Indian stock market. If we compare its composition in 1986 when it was launched, in 1992 when the economic liberalization process had just begun and in December 2023, we will see that only a handful of companies have survived on this prestigious index.

Tata Steel, Tata Motors, Reliance Industries, Hindustan Unilever, Nestle, and L&T, which have created long-term value not only for their owners but also for all their stakeholders, have cemented their positions in the hearts of investors and created billions of dollars of wealth for everyone involved with them. All these companies have established track records and a history of social conscience, and these have contributed to their longevity and success.

On the other hand, companies such as Premier Automobiles and Hindustan Motors, which dominated the domestic Indian passenger car market for almost four decades since the 1950s, did not invest in research and so, could not face the competition from global auto majors that flooded into the country after 1991. Not surprisingly, they are no longer counted among India's blue-chip companies and have gradually faded away.

The BSE Sensex at the end of 2023 has several information technology and banking companies. They are not only profitable and, in most cases, globally competitive, but also very punctilious about their stated purpose of creating value for society and this forms part of their attractiveness to many investors, particularly those that prioritize ethical considerations over short-term gains.

A similar churn will be evident if one compares the Fortune 500 list over the decades. The list, which first appeared in 1955, has only fifty-two of the original companies.

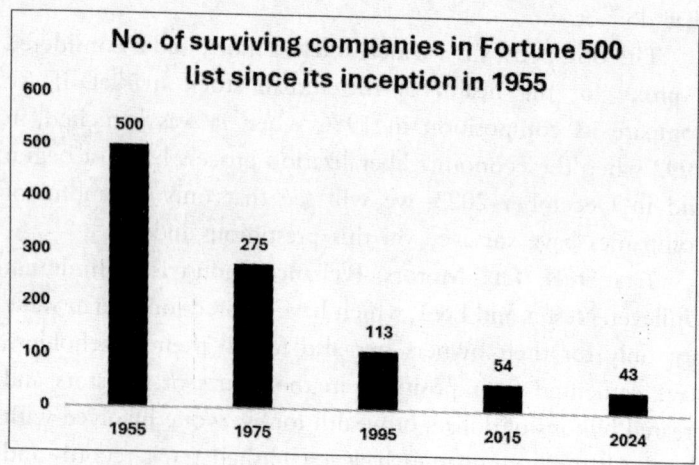

Image 11: The number of companies in the Fortune 500 list has shrunk over the years

The remaining companies have gone bankrupt, merged with others, been taken over, ceased production, or exist in less dominant avatars. This shows how difficult it is for businesses to consistently add value and create wealth over a long period of time. It also shows businesses have to constantly strive to stay ahead of the competition to stay relevant and true to their purpose.

DEFINING PURPOSE

A good way of defining the purpose of a business will be to ask three questions:

> What does the business do?
> How does the business do what it does?
> And why does the business do what it does?

It is the answer to the third question that really defines the purpose of the business. While every business knows the answers to the first two questions, only a few are aware of the third one and those who do distinguish themselves as the long-term winners and wealth creators from others.

Let us take the example of Apple. Even a casual bystander will be able to answer the first question without breaking a sweat. The company makes mobile phones, laptops, tablets, and allied products at price bands that place them at the top end of the market. Every business knows the answer to this question.

The answer to the second question is also not very difficult to find. The company employs some of the best engineers, technologists, product designers and marketers in the world who enable it to design and sell some of the most cutting-edge and desirable consumer products in the world. Its mastery over the technology and knowledge of consumer preferences allows it to stay ahead of its rivals year after year in a market characterized by cut-throat competition. Every successful business can answer this second question quite competently.

It is, however, the answer to the third question that poses difficulties in many cases. If one digs a little deeper, it will be clear that many businesses do not have a ready answer to the question WHY. Yet, it is the most important determinant of the purpose for which the business exists.

As we have seen in Chapter 4, Ford Motor Company founder Henry Ford once said customers would have asked for a faster horse if he had asked them their wish. Instead of doing that, he gave them a mobility solution that changed the way the world travelled. Similarly, Apple wanted to fundamentally change the way people across the planet access technology by providing a seamless interface between users and their devices regardless of age, class, education, geography, and gender.

Traditionally, access to technology has been a major barrier to social, political, and financial empowerment. By packing massive amounts of computing power into its portable devices, Apple and other companies like it have brought a range of services—from banking to healthcare to retail to entertainment—within easy reach of millions of consumers.

Much before the iPhone, Apple's iconic innovation was the music player called iPod, which, in some ways, took forward the legacy of the iconic Sony Walkman. Readers who remember the 1980s will remember the tiny cassette player that first offered consumers the option of listening to music on the move. By doing away with the need to carry cassette tapes, the iPod offered access to a much bigger pool of music with greater convenience. The iPhone took this convenience factor forward by bundling dozens of additional services into one handheld device.

Apple, thus, found its purpose and its route to wealth creation by bridging the gaping chasm between technology companies and the common consumer.

Other examples of companies driven by a larger purpose are Tata, Unilever, HDFC, and Wipro. In the early years of economic liberalization, Tata Group's flagship company Tisco (now Tata Steel) came out with the catchy tagline 'We make people. We also make steel.' It clicked and people believed it because the Tata Group by then had already earned for itself decades of goodwill as an ethical business house that cared for society and put its people ahead of its profits.

The group's founder Jamsetji Nusserwanji Tata said: 'In a free enterprise, the community is not just another stakeholder in the business but is, in fact, the very purpose of its existence.' The group has remained true to this credo for more than 150 years. In the early 1900s, the group introduced the eight-hour workday, provident fund, leave with pay, and gratuity for its employees many decades before these were mandated by law and became the norm.

Not only has the group's social commitment won it legions of admirers and the trust of millions of investors, but it has also brought concrete and quantifiable benefits. In 1978, its trade unions stridently opposed and scuttled attempts by the Janata Party government to nationalize the Tata Group flagship and the town that bears the name of its founder. This is possibly the only instance in Indian history when trade unions have resisted a proposed nationalization of a company because the workers trusted the private management more than the government.

Dr Naresh Trehan's story is similar to this. The founder of Medanta Hospital joined the list of Indian billionaires (as per media reports on 30 November 2023). How did this happen? Investors were rewarding him for providing the country with cutting-edge medical solutions that had remained out of bounds for most people in India till recently. Again, this was another instance of a business living up to its purpose, adding value by solving a problem and, thus, creating wealth as a by-product of doing something else very well. Every business has to eventually serve the society in which it functions, and this defines its purpose and reason to exist.

NOT DEFINING PURPOSE CAN BE FATAL FOR BUSINESSES

For every Apple, Samsung, Tata, Unilever, and Ford, there are dozens of other companies that have failed to deliver returns to their owners and stakeholders because their purpose for being in business—their driving force—has never been clear.

A casual perusal of business newspapers such as the *Economic Times* will show there are dozens of companies that are facing bankruptcy proceedings at any given point in time. In this context, many real estate companies have been in the news because their fortunes intersect so visibly with those of ordinary homebuyers. Many of these companies expanded too fast, others forayed into unrelated areas in which they had no expertise. Yet others were driven by greed and deliberately siphoned out money for the personal benefit of their top management. These companies never focussed on their larger purpose of providing homes to the community. Rather they became vehicles for the pursuit of accumulation of wealth for their owners at the expense of their key stakeholders—customers and partners. This caused their downfall.

There are examples of other companies in other industries as well. A well-known online education services start-up from India that was seen as a potential global leader only a couple of years ago is now in deep trouble, forcing its investors to take large write-downs in value. It is facing lawsuits and investigations alleging diversion of funds and unfair business practices in multiple jurisdictions across the world. This is another example of a business straying from its larger purpose of providing access to education to the masses at affordable prices in the blind pursuit of building scale. Though scale is the path to wealth creation, the pursuit of scale at the expense of the purpose of the business eventually leads to erosion of wealth. This is a live case study that validates this.

DIRECT CORRELATION BETWEEN PURPOSE, LONGEVITY, AND WEALTH CREATION

Although it is possible for businesses to create lots of wealth even in the absence of a larger purpose for their existence, such businesses find it difficult to survive the vagaries of the market and changing consumer preferences over the long term.

That is because businesses that have a clear purpose are able to engender trust and loyalty of customers, employees, vendors, shareholders, and the society they operate in. When stakeholders trust a business and have faith in its management, they patronize it, buy its products and services, invest their money in it, and treat it with high regard. This translates into higher revenues, profits, and therefore wealth creation.

A second advantage that purpose-driven companies have is the ability to attract and retain top talent. As the world becomes increasingly driven by values and as society becomes more conscious of issues like sustainability, professional talent, especially the younger generation, will be drawn to companies with core values that are aligned with their own. GenZ is very particular about the impact their work has on the society. In the knowledge economy that the world is headed towards, the quality of talent will be the key determinant of success and therefore wealth creation.

Businesses that define their purpose beyond immediate financial milestones usually prioritize sustainability and social commitment over short-term profits. This makes eminent business sense as these lead to ethical and responsible behaviour and reduces the risk of legal, regulatory, and reputational risks and challenges that can damage and even debilitate businesses.

Also, businesses that look beyond immediate short-term profits usually invest in innovation, research, and development. This requires long-term vision and patience since every innovation may not be commercially successful and every effort at R&D may not result in a breakthrough. Only businesses that are willing to play the long game with patience and perseverance succeed in this. Such enterprises usually have the resilience and the wherewithal to stay the course longer than others and draw strength from their stated purpose. Therefore, businesses that are driven by their purpose of doing good for society continue to evolve and remain relevant while those that are driven by only numbers and greater market share get commoditized and eventually get phased out.

These purpose-driven businesses usually have a positive social impact on the communities they operate in and this, in turn, burnishes their reputation, which helps them create more wealth for longer periods of time.

Thus, the linkages between value addition, hunger, input, and purpose as drivers of wealth creation become evident at every step of the process. Businesses or individuals that are not anchored to these attributes and, instead, are driven by greed, output, and numbers can create wealth in the short term but fade out over the longer term.

Chapter 8

RISK-TAKING

Risk is the probability that things will not go as per our expectations. Every decision has an element of uncertainty regarding its outcome. When judiciously addressed, risk-taking is the path to wealth creation.

Risk and reward go hand in hand: this is another age-old aphorism that has been passed down the generations. Wealth is the reward in the future for assuming the risk embedded in any decision taken today. Every decision that we make in life, whether personal or professional, has an element of uncertainty regarding its outcome. It could be a relationship or a career choice.

Risk is nothing but the probability of things not going as per our expectations. However, to win, you have to play the game. There cannot be any return without investing. Conventionally, there is a linear relationship between risk and reward. However, measured decision making could help optimize risk for a given reward, whereas sub-optimal decision making could lead to no reward. That is the reason some people are more successful in wealth creation while most are not, since the relationship between the quality of decision and wealth creation is often neglected. Most wealth creators are smarter and not just lucky.

RISK IN LIFE SITUATIONS

As defined above, risk is inherent in every decision we make. It is the potential for adverse outcomes arising from those decisions. At every stage of life, in everything we do, we exercise choices from a menu of options and each of these has certain levels of risk attached to them. If one considers this point a little deeply, one will realize that even the simplest and most mundane actions involve the possibility of an outcome that is not anticipated. There is obviously a risk in the act of charting a path through the unknown.

Take any real-life situation. The only thing that can be said about it with any degree of certainty is that it will be unpredictable, dynamic, and dependent on a number of variables, many of them outside the control of individuals or businesses. Let us take a simple everyday example of crossing a road or even playing a sport. Each of these very mundane actions has a level of risk attached to it. Every day, hundreds of people meet with accidents while crossing roads and the tragic examples of cricketers Raman Lamba and Phil Hughes who passed away on the cricket field after being hit by a cricket ball will remain etched in every sports lover's mind. Fortunately, such accidents are not everyday occurrences, but that in no way reduces the risk inherent in these simple actions.

Although many people are scared of taking risks, it must be borne in mind that risk is not necessarily negative. Addressed properly and assumed judiciously, it becomes the path to growth, prosperity, and wealth creation. If we flip this argument around, we will see that risk-averse individuals are likely to stagnate in life, miss out on growth opportunities, and miss out on the option of exploring the full potential of their abilities.

If Alexander the Great had not taken the risk of stepping out of his native Macedonia, he would never have conquered much of the known world and become immortal as one of history's greatest generals. Then again, had the Tata Group not taken the risk of stepping outside the domestic Indian market, it would never have become the globally recognized multinational it is today.

As they move forward, individuals and businesses come to new crossroads where they have to decide which path they will follow. Each of these decisions is accompanied by different levels of risk, not all of which will be apparent or known at the time of taking the decision. For example, a salaried individual who is doing well in his existing job may receive an offer from a competing company. Any decision he takes will involve a level of risk. Leaving his job and joining the competitor will mean leaving the comfort of a set-up he is familiar with and heading into the unknown. It will also imply leaving behind the equity of trust built with the current stakeholders and rebuilding the trust with a new set of stakeholders in the new organization, which could take its own unpredictable trajectory. Not taking up the offer will mean accepting the status quo even if there are no growth opportunities in the current organization, which could lead to a stagnant career.

The individual will have to carefully weigh all his options before arriving at a decision—to accept the offer, to reject it, or to explore growth opportunities with his current employer. Despite this, there can be no guarantee that the decision he takes will lead to the outcome he desires because of many factors that he may not be aware of or some that may be beyond his ability to control.

There is, therefore, a direct relationship between risk and

reward. In a majority of cases, the higher the risk the greater the reward and vice versa. This is particularly true in the context of wealth creation.

THE EQUATION OF WEALTH

We have seen this equation before: $FV=PV*(1+R)^N$. We will come across this equation quite often in our journey to wealth creation. It simply means the future value of an investment is a function of the present value of the investment, the rate of return, and the time period over which the present value of the investment is deployed.

Wealth creation in all forms can be reduced to this simple formula. Though it looks disarmingly straightforward, it hides a number of complexities within it. That is because no two investment decisions can ever guarantee the same returns. For example, a business that promises a 15 per cent return per annum could face unexpected headwinds and give 5 per cent return one year and 10 per cent the next. Another business that promises the same rate of return, might face unanticipated tailwinds that could improve its rate of returns to 25 per cent. In extreme cases and in bad years, some businesses might even generate negative returns, i.e., their operations may lead to the erosion of wealth.

So, two individuals who invest identical sums of money in the two businesses will get very different returns on their respective investments. This kind of differential returns are quite common in the stock market. It has been observed that very few small investors recognize the initial stages of a bull run. That is usually when seasoned and institutional investors take positions in stocks and stay invested for an extended period. As news of high returns generated by the markets begin to percolate to society via news reports and word of mouth, more and more small and first-time investors enter the market attracted by the prospect of quick returns. But in many cases, history tells us, the bull run is nearing its end by then and beginning to peter out. Therefore, many small investors end up lose their savings in the correction that follows.

This pattern has been seen in bull run after bull run. So, although all investors in the market are taking the risk, the returns they receive can be quite different. This unpredictability of returns is the risk that every investor, whether individual or institutional, first time or seasoned, assumes. The returns that they receive is the reward they get for taking the risk. However, the magnitude of returns is driven by their understanding of the underlying risk and their ability to manage the same.

Even at an institutional level, this risk-reward equation is very much in evidence. Let us take the real-life example of the UB Group, which was, at one time, the world's largest liquor company by volumes. It was the clear market leader in India, miles ahead of its rivals, and had added a feather in its cap by acquiring two major Scotch whisky brands along with all their associated distilling assets and marketing infrastructure in the face of stiff opposition from its global rivals. Then, the group embarked on an expansion plan in an unrelated area—aviation—riding on a very tenuous brand extension of its bestselling beer brand based on the tagline 'King of Good Times'. It offered air travellers a premium experience that was on a par with the best available air travel services anywhere in the world, which was a novelty in the Indian market.

Initially, this brand extension into an area the group had no experience in seemed to work and the new airline received fantastic feedback and reviews from air travellers as well as the media. But the group could not sustain the cash burn involved in setting up an airline from scratch and running it. It soon fell behind in making statutory payments, defaulted on its loans, and finally had to down shutters leaving a trail of broken lives and shattered dreams in its wake. Not only was the airline venture a spectacular failure, but it also dragged the established and profitable liquor business down with it, forcing the promoter to sell to an international rival.

In this case, the risk of expanding into an unrelated business was not worth the reward, and it led to a massive erosion of wealth not only for the promoter but also for legions of investors, employees, and other stakeholders who had invested their trust and hard-earned money in the business. The end result was very different from what the promoter may have envisaged when he set out on this expansion programme. This was, thus, a classic case of assuming a risk that was not well thought through and will go down in the annals of business history as an example of how not to embark on an expansion programme.

There are dozens of such examples in the real estate sector, where companies have expanded their operations at an unsustainable pace. As a result, they have been forced to spread their resources too thinly across too many projects, resulting in a slew of incomplete projects, allegations of fraud, court cases, bankruptcies, and a trail of financial losses leading to erosion of wealth. Therefore, sub-optimal decision-making amplifies risk and leads to undesirable outcomes. This shows that the mitigation of risk is a key responsibility of the management—and success or failure on this count often makes all the difference between wealth creation and wealth erosion.

However, at the same time, it must be emphasized that the above examples should not be taken to mean that businesses should not take any risks. To do so would condemn them to an existence devoid of growth and the opportunity to expand. That will stymie all innovation which will hinder their ability to solve problems, which, as we have seen in previous chapters, is the basic building block of wealth creation. Therefore, risk avoidance is impractical and such a course of action will bring society to a standstill. All progress in history—from the stage of hunter-gatherers to agriculture to trade, industry, and the information age—has been made possible by risk takers and early adopters who ventured into new territories and opened up new vistas of human development.

RISK TAKING IN HUMAN HISTORY

It is now accepted that modern human beings originated in Africa and then spread slowly throughout the globe. The early humans who walked their way up the coast of Africa and wandered into Asia and Europe and then crossed the seas to Australia and the Americas were the original risk takers. They had no knowledge of what lay beyond their line of sight; yet they dared to venture forth and colonize the world, giving rise to nations, nationalities, civilizations, empires, and all the human progress associated with these.

Every empire in history was the result of risk-taking by emperors and their generals. This brought untold wealth to many ancient and modern empires and provided an impetus for the development of science, technology, arts, architecture, and the pursuit of knowledge, beauty, and excellence.

However, when the hunger for expansion crossed over to greed for expansion it turned out to be fatal for empires. Historians use the term 'imperial overreach' to describe the risks taken by empires to expand their horizon beyond their capability. There are dozens of examples of large empires taking risks that were well beyond their ability to assume—and these often set off a series of events that led to their downfall.

The expansion of the Roman empire, its division into the Eastern Roman empire with its capital in Constantinople (now Istanbul), and the Western Roman empire with its capital in Rome, are a prime example of this overreach.

History is proof that humankind has always been driven by the pursuit of expansion and the creation of wealth. History is also full of examples of the risk of not finishing that journey and landing somewhere that had not been anticipated by those who embarked on that journey.

Explorers and adventurers like Christopher Columbus, Ferdinand Magellan, and Vasco da Gama, who discovered new lands by charting new courses were preceded by hundreds of other risk takers who failed.

Like Columbus, Magellan, and da Gama, successful wealth creators are not merely lucky. They are successful because they have studied previous trends, taken judicious risks, and embarked on their journey when the time was opportune.

WEALTH CREATION FROM RISK TAKING IN CONTEMPORARY SOCIETY

We have seen that wealth creators create wealth by solving problems and by adding value to society. Entrepreneurs like Elon Musk of Tesla, Mark Zuckerberg of Meta, Sachin Bansal and Binny Bansal of Flipkart, Bhavish Aggarwal of Ola, and Deepinder Goyal of Zomato have all created enormous wealth from scratch on the strength of the power of their ideas executed well. Their journey which started with one idea went through several iterations and landed them in a promised land that is perhaps very different than anything they had imagined. Their story is not too different from the adventures of the voyagers of history mentioned in the previous section. Therefore, the principle of wealth creation as the reward for assuming measured risk remains a timeless route to wealth creation.

All of them took risks by taking innovative but untested ideas to the market. When they were starting out and had only the seed of an idea, there was always the risk that the market may not accept their idea and that their business venture may not work. This ideation risk had to be addressed by validation, first from customers and then from investors. That is what investors refer to as the proof of concept. A new idea is usually an untested one, so, a trial run is sometimes resorted to. When a pilot project is successful, investors gain conviction that there are customers for the concept and invest their capital to back the idea.

Let us take the examples of carmakers such as Suzuki and General Motors. Both are internationally successful companies; they entered the Indian market at different times. However, while Suzuki is the clear market leader in the Indian passenger car market, General Motors had to withdraw from India as none of the models it launched in the country found favour with the Indian consumer.

Let us take another example—of Apple iPhones. Every few months, the phone maker updates its system software and also upgrades the hardware with a new edition of the phone every few years. The company does this to mitigate the risk of rivals coming up with me-too features on their phones, thereby commoditizing the premium features that distinguish iPhones from the phones manufactured by rival companies.

Five years ago, the pioneers of the electric vehicle industry were taking a big risk by investing in infrastructure to set up assembly plants for EVs because the market was not yet ready for such a product. The infrastructure for charging these vehicles was inadequate and so, buyers had to worry about the distance they could travel. The risk taken by the pioneers of the sector set the stage for the wider adoption of these vehicles. If the sector has reached a position where it is on the verge of take-off, it owes a lot to those risk takers who ventured where many established names had feared to tread.

As we discussed earlier, one cannot reach one's destination without being on the road. Wealth creators are driven by a larger purpose and their hunger leads them to solve problems for society by executing their ideas with diligence and hard work. They are prepared to take the inherent but well informed and understood risks in this process, which enables them to create wealth as the output.

Chapter 9

COMPOUNDING EFFECT

The compounding effect is when small, incremental, and consistent effort over long periods of time result in big outcomes.

Albert Einstein said compound interest is the eighth wonder of the world. While that observation pertained to the financial world, in this chapter we shall examine how the phenomenon of compounding is prevalent universally in all life situations and brings non-linear growth over a longer period of time.

If a business solves problems for the society it operates in with consistency over a long period of time, it develops into a dependable brand. This bond of trustworthiness between the service provider business and the customer brings into play the compounding effect when it starts attracting more work orders from the same customer. In business jargon, this is called a higher share of the wallet. This then spreads to new work from new customers, thus helping the business to scale up its operations. This is the secret formula for growth in all life situations, whether personal or professional. If you have delivered value to your stakeholders in the same organization over a long period of time, you attract more responsibility and with that comes growth in your pay cheque.

Conversely, the inability to stay the course over the

long-term acts as a natural filtration process, which is why we see a pyramid-like structure in organizational charts and in the world around us in general. To become a banyan tree, one has to be rooted in one place over a very long time.

COMPOUNDING EFFECT EXPLAINED

Though most people usually associate compounding with financial returns, a closer look will show it applies to various other aspects of life as well. In every such sphere, the process of compounding exponentially increases the rate of growth over longer periods of time.

Shorn of technical and mathematical jargon, the process of compounding harnesses the power of cumulative growth that builds upon the small incremental growth achieved every minute, every hour, and every day. Over longer periods of times, this cumulative growth adds up to a remarkably high rate of growth that is much higher than the incremental rate of return.

In life situations, the compounding effect is built on the foundation of trust which is earned and then sustained over a long period of time. When a business or a service provider solves problems for its customers consistently over an extended length of time, it builds a track record of delivering value, which helps it to earn the trust of not only its customers but also other stakeholders including its employees and partners. Satisfied customers then help attract new customers and this creates a virtuous circle of goodwill, higher profitability, and growth. This public trust, earned over many years, enables such a business to expand into new markets and extend its brand into related sectors. In this case, the trust earned by the business is the base investment and the reward that it earns in the form of expanded market share, larger top line and higher profits is the compounding effect. This is more than just the transactional nature of business. As word of its credibility spreads far and wide, it creates the foundation for the next phase of growth. That, in a nutshell, explains the power of compounding.

The secret formula mentioned in the introduction to this chapter is the ability to understand, harness, leverage, and exploit the exponential growth opportunities offered by compounding in one's professional and business context. However, readers must bear in mind that one needs lots of patience and very strong nerves to benefit fully from the phenomenon of compounding. Very often, one encounters strong headwinds, severe turbulence, and temporary setbacks en route to one's goals. Many people lose their nerve or run out of patience and abandon their quest for geometric progression. This acts as a natural barrier and filters out the potential winners from the others. Only those who can endure the trials and tribulations of a long journey can enjoy the fruits of reaching the destination. Hasty, impulsive, and knee-jerk reactions, therefore, have to be avoided in order to benefit from the power of compounding.

COMPOUNDING IN PERSONAL SITUATIONS

Compounding works just as effectively in personal situations as it does in professional ones. We must always remember that it applies to every sphere of life. It is the lifeblood of enduring relationships built on the foundation of mutual trust. The element of trust, which is the lynchpin of the entire compounding process, can never be built overnight. It is the effect of long years of toil, loyalty, grit, integrity, and delivery. So, incorporating all these attributes into our lives is a necessary pre-condition to being able to harness the power of compounding in personal situations leading to wealth creation.

Let us first try and understand how compounding affects our day-to-day lives and how we encounter it in everyday situations. It affects every aspect of our lives—like the relationships that we build with family and friends over decades. While supportive families show unconditional support (unfortunately, not everyone is lucky enough to have this), close and true friends show up in situations of medical emergency, financial support, or even as a sounding board for taking critical life decisions like choosing a career, accepting a job offer, or even finalizing a life or a business partner. Compounding is also evident where our health is concerned. An illness or medical problem when ignored could grow into such a large issue as to need surgery or long-term treatment. Conversely, if one takes care of all aspects of well-being: nutrition, physical, mental/emotional health, they combine over many months and years to ensure a healthy life. Similarly, education does not stop after graduating from schools and colleges. It is a lifelong journey and the real education from the university of life only begins the day formal education comes to an end.

From these examples, it will be evident that small but consistent incremental efforts invested over a very long period of time is the root of all success stories. In every case, it will be clear that success is never the immediate result of one-time input. Rather, layers of the repeat inputs applied consistently over a period of many years are needed to produce a scholar academician, a champion sportsperson, or a maestro musician. That is how the power of compounding works. Internalizing this knowledge can prepare us to face most life situations better and develop the endurance to stay in the game even when each individual step looks difficult, and the goal seems distant and out of reach.

COMPOUNDING IN THE PROFESSIONAL CONTEXT

The effects of compounding are equally apparent in the workplace too. Very often, we come across individuals and companies that have transformed their own lives and those of their stakeholders by delivering consistent value over extended periods of time. In the process, they have taken their own reputation and that of their employers to greater heights by leveraging the power of compounding.

Given below are some examples:

Professional skill development: When companies hire for new functions, they are looking for particular sets of skills. Individuals having the required skills stand a good chance of getting hired for such career openings. Some of these individuals have invested in themselves to acquire the skills required by employers after undergoing rigorous training despite having other pre-existing professional qualifications. Every new certification may not have brought any immediate rewards in their professional lives but over time, the cumulative effect of their incremental experience and qualifications bears fruit and they are able to climb up the professional ladder, with a bigger role and financial rewards.

There are enough examples of this in the world of sports as well. Sachin Tendulkar has said on record that he often spent as much as twelve hours a day on the field practising his craft and perfecting his game in preparation for when he turned out for India. This long-term commitment to excellence is what sets champions apart.

Similarly, commercial pilots have to log a minimum of 250 hours of flying time, of which 100 hours have to be in powered aircraft and 100 hours as pilot-in-command time. To become a captain of a commercial aircraft, one must log at least 1,500 flight hours and hold a full Air Transport Pilot's License. However, most airlines promote pilots to captain only after they log at least 3,000 flight hours. IT professionals also add skills like artificial intelligence, machine learning, and big data analytics to their existing qualifications to stay relevant for the future. In each of these instances, people are adding layers of knowledge and skills to a pre-existing level of expertise to become even more valuable to the buyer of their services over a long period of time. This is the power of compounding.

Fund Management: The same effect of compounding is visible in the career graphs of successful fund managers. Let us take the example of Prashant Jain, who has been among India's most successful and admired fund managers. Jain was the Chief Investment Officer at HDFC Mutual Fund from 2004 to 2022. He is the only fund manager in India to have continuously managed a fund for 28 years. This fund, which is now known as HDFC Balanced Advantage Fund, was a hybrid equity and debt fund and delivered a compounded average growth rate (CAGR) of 17.9 per cent between January 1994 and July 2022 as against 9.6 per cent delivered by Sensex. This track record stands out because the Sensex is 100 per cent equity while Jain's fund was on average 65 per cent equity and 35 per cent debt. Jain was able to deliver almost double the returns of Sensex with only two-thirds exposure to equity. Every ₹100 invested in the fund had grown to ₹10,940 which is 109 times over 28 years. Investors flocked and stayed loyal to Jain's fund in particular and HDFC Mutual Fund in general on account of this compelling performance. During his tenure, HDFC Balanced Advantage Fund grew to ₹46,000 core while HDFC Mutual Funds Assets under management grew from ₹3,000 crore to ₹4,40,000 crore.

Entrepreneurship: A similar compounding effect can be seen in the case of start-up founders who go on to become serial entrepreneurs. These are founders who have built a track record of building successful businesses by converting an idea into reality. By doing so they have proven their abilities to not only come up with innovative ideas for the market but also have monetized them by impeccable execution. They are able to attract investors who are ready to bet on them from Day 1 and throughout their journey of building the business as repeat investors.

For example, Mukesh Bansal, one of India's most successful serial entrepreneurs, founded Myntra, a leading online fashion platform, in 2007 which he sold to Flipkart in 2014 for ₹2,000 crore. It was the biggest acquisition in the Indian e-commerce market at that time. Thereafter, in 2016, he founded CureFit, a health and fitness start-up, which expanded into the realm of mental health and wellness with MindFit and then the online health food delivery business with EatFit. The compounding effect is visible from the trust and faith that leading investors such as Accel Partners, Kalaari Capital, and IDG ventures placed in Bansal by investing first in Myntra and later in CureFit.

Professional Networking: Most networks begin as small informal groups of individuals who help each other out on work-related issues. Over time, the number of individuals in the group grows as interactions with and additions of new individuals add heft to the pre-existing group. Every such interaction adds to the growth of the network. With time, members also develop familiarity, trust, and respect for each other, and this transforms the group of individuals into a powerful professional network that can become a force multiplier for all its members. Such networks are invaluable for referrals, new business opportunities, formal and informal collaborations, and troubleshooting, and can impact one's professional journey positively in many different ways. It is said that one's net worth is a function of one's network. The first and last rule of building a rewarding network is to give to the network instead of trying to benefit from networking. While the latter is a more transactional and opportunistic approach, the former can happen only over a prolonged period of time and when that happens, the compounding effect of the power of your vast network combined with your personal credibility starts paying you back in unimaginable ways.

Leadership Opportunities: We have learnt earlier from the chapter on adding value for wealth creation that the secret to building a rewarding career is adding value to your immediate stakeholders, which could be your peers and immediate seniors, by delivering as expected on every task that is given to you. This helps you build your credibility as someone who could be trusted to deliver on responsibilities, which then helps to bring greater responsibilities your way leading to the expansion of your role thus helping you climb the pyramidical corporate ladder. Consistent delivery on an ever-increasing job role over an exceedingly long period of time helps you build equity of trust with the organizational stakeholders at the leadership level making you a compelling candidate for leading the organization in the future.

One of the most remarkable case studies which validates this is that of Natarajan Chandrasekaran, who without any ties to the Tata family, grew from a junior employee to become the chairman of India's largest business conglomerate. He studied in a government school in Tamil Nadu and received his bachelor's degree in applied sciences from the Coimbatore Institute of Technology in Tamil Nadu. After this, Chandra obtained a master's degree in computer applications from the Regional Engineering College, Tiruchirappalli, before joining TCS as an entry-level employee in 1987. From there, he rose, without any fancy Ivy League degree or family connections, to the position of CEO of TCS in 2009. The crowning glory of his career was his appointment as Chairman of Tata Sons, the holding company of the Tata Group, in January 2017, becoming the first professional and the first non-Parsi to hold that coveted position in the entire history of the Tata Group. He achieved this by delivering results at every stage of his journey with the Tata Group, thus, showcasing the power of compounding over the long term in the professional sphere.

COMPOUNDING AND WEALTH CREATION

We have learnt from examples of compounding effect in both personal and professional situations that if there is one single attribute that brings out the power of compounding, it is trust. While trust gets built over a period of time, it deepens only over an exceedingly long period of time on account of consistent delivery without any adverse surprises. That is when the compounding effect starts showing up. At a personal level, one builds trust with immediate stakeholders like family, friends, and neighbours, and in professional situations, one builds trust with immediate stakeholders like colleagues, employees, customers, partners, and investors. No one can ever be completely self-made because no one lives in a cocoon shielded from all outside influences. One succeeds in creating wealth only because of the bridges built with, and contributions from, immediate stakeholders—both personal and professional. Life is a canvas of collaborations and not a solo journey.

As we've seen, compounding is not limited to the world of financial markets alone, but, in fact, is pervasive across all life situations. Wealth creation is an outcome of the trust built with various stakeholders over a long period of time.

Readers will note that the essence of compounding in wealth creation challenges the notion of success being the result of only one person's efforts. By its very definition, wealth creation is the result of successful collaborations between various stakeholders. It is critically dependent on the bridges that individuals and organizations have built in the past and highlights the importance of teamwork and partnerships in the journey towards wealth creation.

BUILDING A BRAND

Have you ever wondered why the IITs attract lakhs of young aspirants who sit for the entrance examinations every year? At a superficial level, they want to become engineers but if one thinks a little deeper, one will realize that the brand equity associated with the IITs is the result of decades of excellence in churning out world-class engineers.

Every institution is known by the quality of its alumni and in the case of the IITs, it is the alumni that has built the reputation of the institution. It creates a virtuous effect of being able to attract the brightest students, which creates the top-quality peer group on campus and forms a top-quality cohort of alumni that go on to create wealth in their professional lives. Many of them return to give a part of their wealth as a mark of gratitude towards their alma mater. We have seen in the earlier chapter how top Ivy League colleges in the US have accumulated huge endowment funds over the decades, which is nothing but a visible manifestation+ of the compounding effect.

Similarly, one sees successful individuals such as Sundar Pichai of Google and Satya Nadella of Microsoft, who have built their personal brand equity by adding value to their employers and solving problems for the entire duration of their professional lives. Their current positions at the top of their respective corporate pyramids are the result of compounding over many decades. Three decades ago, who would have bet on these two middle class boys from India heading two of the world's greatest wealth creators?

Pichai, an IIT alumnus, joined Google in 2004 as vice president of Product Development focused on Google's Toolbar. One of his early achievements was convincing co-founders Larry Page and Sergey Brin of the need to build Google's own browser, Chrome, which is now the world's most popular browser. According to Bloomberg, Pichai was well liked and his focus on results led to him being given greater responsibilities. In 2013, he was promoted to head the company's Android division. Thereafter, he was given charge of Google+, Maps, Search, commerce, ads, and infrastructure, thus, cementing his position as the executive to watch out for. In August 2015, Sundar Pichai was appointed CEO of the company—the culmination of his track record of delivering value consistently over a long period of time. He could be trusted to lead Google, which he has done remarkably well ever since.

Satya Nadella, an engineer from the Manipal Institute of Technology, joined Microsoft in 1992, and came into prominence for shaping the company's cloud computing strategy, which has contributed significantly to its success. As Senior Vice President of R&D at the company's online services department, he guided the development of Bing, Microsoft's search engine. Then, as Executive Vice President of the company's Cloud & Enterprise Division, Nadella led the growth of the company's cloud business that has been responsible for much of its growth in recent years. Given his long track record on delivering growth, it did not come as a complete surprise when he was named CEO in 2014 after twenty-two years at Microsoft.

Have you ever wondered why we see a pyramid-like structure in the society and the world around us related to wealth creation and its ownership? That is because not everyone is able to stay invested in the marathon of life. Like physical endurance in a marathon race, life's marathon requires emotional endurance—and not everyone can last the distance. Compounding effect in life situations shows up by doing the same thing extremely well over a very long period of time. No wonder Einstein called it the eighth wonder of the world.

Chapter 10

LEARNING FROM FAILING AND SUCCEEDING

Failures tell us what not to do and successes teach us what to do more of. Wealth creation is about adaptability and lifelong learning—the more adaptable one is, the more likely one is to create wealth.

The University of Life teaches us that while all successful people have experienced failure, real appreciation for excellence comes only when one experiences success. Both failure and success are teachers—one tells us what not to do and the other teaches us what to do and do more and more of.

One cannot become a successful entrepreneur without failing in a couple of ventures or tweaking one's business model to adapt to the changing market dynamics. One cannot become a successful investor without making investment mistakes. Likewise, both these successful individuals also know which buttons to push more and more. Wealth creation is all about constant evolution, adaptation, and on-the-job learning.

THE PRINCIPLE OF ADAPTABILITY

Experiencing success and failure teaches us what works and what does not. Wealth creation is about adaptation and lifelong learning—the more adaptable one is, the more likely one is to create wealth.

Adaptability is the capacity of all living beings to adjust to changes in the external or internal environments. It is a fundamental law of creation and is visible in all spheres of life—within the family, at work, on the sports field, in friendships, and even in plant and animal life. As Charles Darwin discovered, it is not the smartest and the strongest that survive but those that are most adaptable to change. Survival is a prerequisite for wealth creation—one wins a war only if one lives. Similarly, one creates wealth only if one survives the pulls and pressures of the ever-changing business environment, the information asymmetry that entrepreneurs and investors have to live with, and the moves of competitors. It takes great agility of mind, flexibility of response, and adaptability to survive and prosper in such an environment. Adaptability is, therefore, not just a desirable attribute but a necessary precondition for success in any venture.

It is only by carefully analysing the decisions and the steps that led to failure that we can identify and isolate the causes that led to the failure. Then, a careful consideration of options and alternative courses of action will reveal new ways of addressing the problem at hand and lead to the desired solution and result in success. Adaptability is the ability to identify the mistakes, the search for new ways of solving problems, tweak and refine existing methods of doing things, and developing the new skills necessary to execute the solution.

Consider any real-life situation and you will see the above formula at play. Successful entrepreneurs and investors display an agility of response and the ability to modify their thought process when faced with obstacles in their path to success. As we have seen in the chapter on risk, all life situations are fraught with uncertainties and the outcomes could be very different from those that we envisage. Success in business depends not only on decisions taken by the entrepreneur but also on the wider economic, political, and social developments that are beyond the ability of any individual to control. But even if one cannot always control the external environment, it is possible to make the best use of it—or at least restrict the damage it can cause—by displaying the ability to think on one's feet and adapting to the fast-changing situation.

One should always bear in mind that successful entrepreneurs are not necessarily immune to bad decisions and losses. Rather, they are like sailors who know when to roll back their sails to avoid damage during storms and then unfurl them when the winds turn favourable again.

And this is an explanation for a critical aspect of the wealth creation formula—the ability of some individuals to overcome the odds and sashay their way to success even as many others give up the quest midway through their journey. That magic attribute is adaptability.

ADAPTABILITY IN EVERYDAY LIFE

All living beings are born with an inherent ability to adapt to their environment. However, some beings display a greater ability to survive and thrive in adverse situations than others. What differentiates the two types of personalities is the ability, inclination, and appetite of the former to constantly learn, unlearn, and relearn lessons that life keeps teaching all of us.

Let us take an example that many of us will be familiar with. In many middle-class Indian families, it is the norm to expect children to take admission to an engineering or a medical college, or take coaching to qualify for the all-India civil services. Every year, millions of aspirants start out on this journey but only a handful reach their goal. But it is not as if all the individuals who fail to become engineers and doctors or IAS and IPS officers fall by the wayside of life. There are several inspiring stories of young men and women who failed to enter the profession of their choice or realized midway that they would rather be doing something else, changed course, adapted, charted a new direction, and made a success of their life.

Every year, thousands of students change streams from science to commerce to humanities when they realize that a maths-heavy syllabus is not for them. Many such students blossom in the more creative subjects that the humanities stream offers. These are examples of adaptability in everyday, non-business situations.

Let us take another example. The restaurant industry faced an existential challenge during the peak of the Covid-19 pandemic. With patrons unwilling to risk physical attendance at restaurants, some restaurateurs saw an opportunity to address a much bigger market by delivering food to the homes of customers—rather than the limited number that could be fed in the restaurant. Those who moved to the delivery model thrived while many of those who could not adapt had to shut shop.

The print media also faced a challenge with the advent of the television industry and later, both the print and the audio-visual media were challenged by the digital media sector. Some media groups adapted by setting up their own TV channels. Then, most media groups now have digital platforms, which allow them to reach a much bigger audience than printed newspapers and magazines could hope to reach.

Life is all about choices and the need to shuffle between them. Typically, people like to repeat their good experiences and move on from their bad ones. This is why some brands endure over generations while others find it difficult to establish themselves in the hearts and minds of consumers. The key distinction between the long-term winners and the others is the adaptability of some brands compared to their peers and rivals.

It will be evident from the above that adaptability is not a static concept, but a dynamic process fuelled by a combination of everyday experiences, macro factors, and the inclinations of the people involved in the process. A crucial aspect of adaptability is having a growth-oriented mindset. It tells us about our strengths and weaknesses and this, in turn, propels us to take some actions and avoid others so as to increase our chances of success.

Adaptability is, thus, a critical life force that powers all living beings in this world.

RISING FROM THE ASHES

Adaptability is the ability to take reverses in your stride, draw the right lessons from them, and then do less and less of the things that led to the failure. It also involves modifying one's response to a given stimulus to increase the chances of success.

Rare is the successful individual who has not failed before tasting success. It has rightly been said that you only rise after falling. So, someone who has not seen failure will rarely become conspicuously successful. What is true for individuals is equally true for businesses, institutions, and countries as well.

Singapore offers a classic example of adaptability powering a poor city state with very limited resources to the high table of the global comity of nations. A former Crown colony of the British Empire, it gained self-governance in 1959 and four years later, merged into the newly created Federation of Malaysia along with the states of Malaya, North Borneo, and

Sarawak. This merger, however, did not proceed as smoothly as envisaged, and bitter disputes arose between Singapore and the other constituent states of Malaysia. Finally, matters came to a head in 1965 when Singapore was expelled from the Malaysian federation.

Singapore was independent but orphaned. The tiny city state, with one of the highest population densities in the world, did not have many natural resources, it had a diverse and not very literate population, and the future looked rather bleak. But its new prime minister Lee Kuan Yew was not a man to be cowed by circumstances. Displaying adaptability that would become a global case study for good governance and visionary leadership, he embarked on a series of steps to first educate his people, provide them housing, teach them new skills, and position his fledgling city state as a global free trade hub that would transform that tiny South East Asian backwater into a global centre of trade, finance, fashion, and tourism rivalling London and New York—all in the space of one generation.

The scale of its achievement will be apparent if one compares its performance to that of its neighbours—many of them have managed to improve the lives of their citizens but none has attained the heights attained by Singapore. The primary reason for this was the adaptability it displayed in adopting policies and positioning itself to take maximum advantage of the changing patterns of global trade and tourism flows. These, and a carefully calibrated reorientation of its social and cultural practices enabled it to ride the global trade winds to deliver a very high quality of life to all its citizens. Its neighbours, that adapted less well to the changing tides of the post–World War II order, could not achieve the same level of development and financial prosperity.

Similarly, countries like Germany and Japan, which had

been ruined during World War II, learnt the right lessons, eschewed military spending in the post-War years, and focused all their attention on rebuilding their economies. Instead of giving in to despair, they embarked on a journey of re-education of their populations, focused on innovation and technological breakthroughs. This adaptability enabled them to overcome the terrible devastation and bounce back to the top echelons of the world's economic rankings within a few decades.

Even iconic start-up founders such as Steve Jobs, Jack Ma, and Elon Musk, among others, have had to face near debilitating setbacks in their careers that would have broken lesser men. But by dipping into reserves of adaptability that only the most successful people possess, they turned their fortunes around and emblazoned their names in the annals of business history.

Steve Jobs had been ousted from Apple and spent many years outside the company, during which he founded NeXT and Pixar. They contributed significantly to his success and aura as an entrepreneur and set the stage for his triumphant return to Apple and the launch of a raft of pathbreaking products such as the iPod, iPhone, and iPad, among others. Then, Jack Ma's first business venture, an online directory for Chinese businesses, failed to take off. Unfazed by this failure, he analysed its shortcomings, adapted his responses, and launched Alibaba, the company that made him a household name across the globe. Elon Musk's lack of success with ventures like Zip2 and X.com (which later became famous as PayPal) taught him how to adapt to the fast-changing world of business and technology and prepared him for his subsequent tryst with success in the form of Tesla and SpaceX.

These examples teach us that every individual, company,

or country can succeed even in the face of extreme odds if it is willing to adapt and learn the right lessons from its failures.

ADAPTABILITY AND SUCCESS

Darwin's theory of natural selection tells us that the most adaptable of the species, rather than the strongest or the cleverest, survive. This is true of entire species of sportspersons, businesspeople, and wealth creators as well.

Most cricket fans will recall images of cricketer Virat Kohli from his days as a teenage sensation. He was, even then, an individual of prodigious talent. Most pundits predicted a bright future ahead of him. He was then, however, not the fittest or the most athletic junior cricketer around. With cricket leagues mushrooming all over the world, the game was fast becoming a 24x7x365 vocation for its practitioners, where one needed to be very fit to survive against the best in the world. Young Kohli adapted to this changing world, altered his diet completely, dedicated himself to physical fitness and emerged within a short time as the global poster boy of cricket fitness—so much so that even foreign players, thus far the standard bearers of athleticism and fitness, now look to him for inspiration when it comes to remaining in shape. This adaptability is what distinguishes champion sportspersons from others who also play the game and is a critical determinant of success not only in sports but in every other sphere of life.

In India, everyone is familiar with the names of business houses such as Tata and Birla. These groups survived stiff competition from British firms during the era of British India, then endured the hostile business environment created by the adoption of socialism as the official government credo in independent India, and thrived in the free-market regime ushered in by the 1991 economic liberalization programme. Along the way, they have evolved from jute and cotton textile merchants to industrialists making steel, automobiles, cement, carbon black, aluminium, rayon, fertilizers, salt, software, consumer goods to even offering financial services, telecom services, electric power, and hospitality services. The secret behind their longevity and success is their ability to adapt to different policy regimes and political environments not only in India but in every continent of the world where they are now present. They understand the markets they operate in better than most others and keep tweaking their responses to improve their chances of survival. Thus, adaptability is the key reason for their continued success.

ROLE OF HUMILITY IN ADAPTABILITY AND WEALTH CREATION

Past successes can never guarantee similar results in the future. That is because circumstances change, consumer tastes evolve, new technologies are developed, and society moves on from the old order, which yields place to the new. The only way to survive and thrive in this ever-changing landscape is to keep learning new things, evolving with the times, and adapting to the transformed environment.

Under the circumstances, it is very important to have the humility to acknowledge that one does not know everything and that even the masters of the game have to learn new methods of solving existing problems in order to stay a step ahead of one's rivals. Thus, learning and relearning is an ongoing journey that never stops. In the journey towards wealth creation, one must humbly accept that the most successful techniques of today will become dated and commoditized tomorrow.

One must also have the humility to realize that the market is always right and that we, as wealth creators, must always keep learning new lessons from it.

Humility is the key to have an open mind since it does not let you believe that you know everything. You are ever open to learn from the environment around you. Developing an agile and open mind that adapts quickly to any new stimulus is, thus, the best way to stay ahead of the curve much needed for wealth creation.

Chapter 11

SHOWING UP IN LIFE

Even the best player in the world cannot win a match by sitting on the sidelines.

No one wins a match without being on the playground. Wealth creation, too, is the by-product of going through the process of being there and doing what needs to be done when it needs to be done. Lucky are those who act to execute their plans to convert their dreams into reality. They are always on the lookout for what is next and are the first ones to know about new skills to be acquired, new opportunities that may be there in the market, new and better ways to solve the same problem and so on. A farmer who is on his farm every day knows what his crop needs next; a business owner who is on the floor daily or is meeting customers regularly knows what his business needs next. Wealth comes only to those who are alive and alive are those who are active.

Mere existence is not enough to ensure success. One has to actively engage with one's surroundings and circumstances and proactively take on the challenges that life throws one's way.

Action, therefore, lies at the core of the concept of 'showing up'. Success is the by-product and end result of concerted action. For example, attending a social event might qualify as 'showing up' in the social sense but will not, by itself, bring any social capital or other benefits. The 'action' involves networking with those present at the gathering, building bridges, finding common areas of interest, and leveraging the connection(s) made for mutual benefit. Similarly, one can play a game only if one shows up at the playground. Being the best player in the world will not count for much if one is sitting on the sidelines and watching the game from outside rather than actively participating in it. Then, a highly rated young player on the periphery of the national side will never make it to the team if he/she is not present at pre-selection trials. The player increases the chances of being selected by 'showing up'. Here, too, merely marking a presence will not suffice. The player will also have to prove his/her mettle to the selectors.

Thus, showing up can be defined as a mindset, an approach that signals willingness to face the ups and downs that everyone has to encounter at every step of life—whether in the realm of family or friendships, job or business, sports or hobby. It is only by showing up that one can honestly gauge one's readiness for the battles that lie ahead. It enables individuals, teams, and companies to assess the level of their readiness to face challenges, identify gap areas, and suggest areas of improvement. Those who 'show up' also realize over time that progress towards a given goal is often not linear but involves a stop-start journey in which several obstacles have to be overcome and roadblocks removed.

An area sales manager in an FMCG company, for example, is usually mandated to oversee channel sales—a chain of stockists, distributors, and retailers through which the product travels to get from the manufacturer to the end consumer. It is his/her job to ensure that the company's merchandise is displayed prominently on the shelves of retailers, that distributors are addressing the issues faced by the channel and that customer feedback is being relayed honestly to the decision makers in the company in good time. To do this, the manager will have to be keep his/her ear to the ground. The best way of doing so will be to go on regular tours of their territory and get first hand reports from the ground. In today's data-heavy age and extensive Management Information System (MIS) reporting systems, it is possible for managers sitting at the head office to get a lot of this information from the comfort of their airconditioned offices, but only the manager who 'shows up' on the ground will be able to catch the pulse of the customer and the retailer as well as the sight of the competitor's products vying for the attention of the same customer on the same shelf. These convey a reality that no Power Point presentation can capture.

In the manufacturing sector, too, the role of the production manager is of paramount importance. Effective production managers 'show up' by making regular physical visits to the shop floor for first-hand accounts of the conditions prevailing there. He/she interacts with workers to assess the morale of the workforce and the challenges faced by them. All the secondary data that is captured in various data sets can be reported to superiors sitting in remote locations, but only the person on the ground gets the 'feel' of the shop floor and can make sense of the intangible sentiments that often make a big difference between success and mediocrity.

Even on battlefields, the legendary officers, commanders, and generals are those who lead their troops from the front on the ground. They are the military leaders who become decorated soldiers and folk heroes who continue to inspire others long after the war is over.

EXAMPLES FROM EVERYDAY LIFE

Showing up is key to succeeding in real-life situations—be it in the realms of education, business and entrepreneurship, corporate career, sports, or investing.

Education: In the field of education, showing up is not merely attending classes and marking attendance. It is demonstrating the thirst for knowledge, the determination to go beyond the immediate question at hand to figure out why something happened in a particular way, to find an articulate way of answering a question, and engaging in a lifelong quest of enquiry and discovery that broadens one's horizons and enlarges one's reservoir of knowledge.

In most classes, there are three categories of students. The first category will attend all lectures, collect all the notes but will rarely go beyond the books. Their goal is to clear the examinations, which they do as expected from any student. The second category of students is often absent from class. They spend most of their time in other pursuits and wake up just before their examinations. Only some of these students pass their tests; others fail and drop out. The last category comprises students for whom schools and colleges are all about learning, not just from their textbooks, but also from extra-curricular work and from participating in sports.

Good students use opportunities such as these to pick up invaluable life skills like teamwork, how to win within the remit of the rules, and sportsmanship. It is also an opportunity to build networks that will stay with them through their education and professional careers. All these are learnings from beyond the scope of academics but form a critical part of one's education and hold the key to character formation.

Only students who 'show up' beyond the classroom learn these extraordinary life lessons and, thus, are able to create lives that are beyond the ordinary. It is important to note that no teacher or set curriculum can teach students these lessons. One picks them up only by showing up.

Business and Entrepreneurship: For business owners, showing up would mean keeping an ear to the ground to pick up the subtle signals from the market and proactively responding to them. In today's context, it would probably include being active in one's industry association, actively representing one's industry at networking sessions, and engaging constructively with peers and competitors in order to stay abreast of the latest developments. It also helps if one stays proactively focused on the evolving needs of customers. Not only do these help raise one's own profile within the peer group, they also give one's brand a visibility that could become a key determinant of success. Having a sense of the emerging trends helps the business owner stay ahead of the competition, tap into talent networks with the requisite skills, and give customers the solutions they want. These are the critical components of success in the ultra-competitive world of business and are available only to those who 'show up'.

Going a step forward, modern-day entrepreneurs have to make pitches to investors for which they have to reach out to the investor networks and show up in front of potential investors to make their passionate pitches. The first set of investors who could be willing to back the idea of the venture at the ideation stage are usually friends and family who know the entrepreneur and can trust him with the start-up capital. Next, the entrepreneur has to show up by demonstrating the proof of concept with real customers in a pilot project. Once that is done, the entrepreneur has to show up to raise the next round of funding from institutional investors like seed or early-stage funds. This journey of showing up before relevant stakeholders has to continue as the business scales from an early stage to growth stage to an IPO. This has been the journey of many of today's giant corporations such as Meta, Google, Amazon, Netflix, Zomato, and Ola to name a few. They grew from the seed of an idea in an entrepreneur's mind to multibillion-dollar companies. These success stories did not happen in a vacuum. These companies attained their iconic status because their founders showed up and were ready to be counted when it mattered.

Corporate Career: One will also see the difference between those who are only physically present and those who show up in any office or professional situation. For most people, a job is something they have to do to earn money to sustain themselves. They log in at the office at 10 a.m. every weekday and log out at 6 p.m., and in most cases meet the expectations of their employer. Such people usually retain their jobs and experience career progression at a moderate pace. Look around, and a majority of people you see will fall into this category. Then, there is a small percentage of people who do not perform as per expectations. Such people are soon identified and get filtered out of the system.

There is, however, a third group of executives who will take the initiative to reach the office much before time, find things to do beyond the call of their duty, not constrained by the limitations of the working hours stipulated by their contracts, and soon make themselves invaluable to their superiors. These executives give themselves greater exposure to industry trends, attend team events and festivities inside and outside office, help add value to their departments and peer groups, and consistently deliver above expectation. Their dynamism is usually rewarded, and they are marked out for fast-track growth on the base of the trust that they build with their stakeholders—their colleagues and the organization. As they deliver beyond and more at each level of organizational responsibility they are promoted to the next level, thus, climbing the ladder of corporate growth while others either get filtered or saturated in their roles. This highlights the pyramidical structure where only those who show up rise to the next level.

Sports: Showing up is also a key ingredient of success in sports. Consider any cricket team. It will comprise a core group of players who know their position in the team and will usually perform as per expectations. These players, like the corporate executives who experience moderate career progression, will seldom set the stadium on fire or be the top draw for fans who flock to the stadiums to watch their favourite team play. Then, there are some players who fail to perform as per expectations and are dropped from the team. Finally, there is a small group of players who go beyond their role and become matchwinners. They establish their reputation by performing consistently in challenging conditions. Their presence in the team lifts the morale of their teammates and deflates that of their opponents. Such players are difficult to replace because they play not just to retain their place in the side, but to make their teams win. These great players go on to become legends, which happens only by showing up as match winners for their teams. They are able to earn and keep the trust and respect of their teammates, fans, and the sports administrations. Such players announce their own retirements and continue to play as long as they feel they can be the match winners for their teams. Coaching camps and training alone cannot make such champions. They 'show up' in good times or bad to lift their teams to attain such a status.

Investing: The markets are dynamic entities that are influenced by multiple factors such as macro-economic parameters—GDP growth, inflation, fiscal deficit, current account deficit, and revenue surpluses/deficits—rainfall data, floods and natural disasters, liquidity situation in the domestic and global markets, geo-political conflicts, and domestic political developments, among others. Everyone with access to the internet will have access to these data sets as they are publicly available. Yet, there are ace investors who are followed and there are others whom few people have heard of. The former are those investors who make the effort to 'show up'. Using their proprietary research and analysis, they create an information arbitrage, which gives them an understanding of the markets that is not available to others. If everybody has access to the same information, then logically, everyone should arrive at the same decisions on buying or selling a stock at the same time. But that is not what happens in the stock market. It is by leveraging the information arbitrage at their disposal that they stay ahead of other investors.

For example, the thirty companies that constitute the BSE Sensex are on the radar of every equity analyst in the market. Everyone has access to all the information about these businesses almost at the same time. Therefore, it may not be possible to discover something different or new for any investor following these companies that might lead to multi-bagger gains. So, many analysts move to the next lot of companies below the level of the largest ones. When this level becomes saturated, they move down the pyramid to the mid-caps, small-caps, and even micro-caps to try and find the hidden jewels that are yet to be discovered by anyone. Some of these could then turn out to be multi-baggers as they are discovered by a broader set of analysts and investors who want to own a piece of the pie. Success in investing is all about taking decisions ahead of others, which can only happen if the investor shows up to find and understand investing opportunities unknown to the rest of the world.

In all the above situations, wealth creation is a by-product of 'showing up'. If there is one phenomenon that is visibly evident in each of these cases it is the pyramidical structure that is everywhere. Whether one is a student, business owner, entrepreneur, corporate executive, athlete, or investor, not everyone is able to make the cut. Only those who show up and are a cut above the rest are able to get to the top of their craft and game. They are the ones who end up creating wealth by either getting picked up by top firms from their campuses, creating a unicorn, getting promoted to the top management, getting a battery of celebrity endorsements or multi-bagger returns.

INHERITORS ALSO HAVE TO SHOW UP

There is a feeling that showing up for wealth creation does not apply to inheritors as they have wealth bequeathed to them by the lottery of birth. It might seem counterfactual, but the rule is very relevant for inheritors. The only difference is their starting baseline. First-generation entrepreneurs usually start with very little, so it takes them a while to earn sufficient capital to create the critical mass necessary for take-off. Inheritors, on the other hand, start with an advantage—of having capital and in most cases a pre-existing network and the infrastructure to perpetuate the success of the preceding generation. But make no mistake. The inheritor starts his/her journey from a higher base but still has to 'show up' to prove himself/herself worthy of the inheritance. There are several instances of inheritors who have expanded their inherited companies into billion-dollar enterprises.

Ratan Tata, Kumar Mangalam Birla, and Mukesh Ambani are three business leaders who inherited large billion-dollar enterprises and built them into multibillion-dollar global conglomerates that compete every day with the best companies around the world.

Ratan Tata was appointed Chairman of Tata Sons, which made him head of the sprawling Tata Group, on the retirement of J. R. D. Tata in 1991. Initially, he faced great resistance from the heads of various operating companies who had been given a lot of freedom by his predecessor. He consolidated his position in a few years and then set about on a global expansion drive that transformed the Tatas from a mainly India-focused business group to a genuinely global conglomerate, which now generates 65 per cent of its sales from overseas markets. In his twenty-one years as chairman, the Tata Group's revenues grew over forty times and profits more than fifty times. He also set the stage for Indian businesses to think globally by taking over Tetley Tea, Corus Steel, and Jaguar Land Rover, thus, placing the Tata Group squarely at the front and centre of India's globalization ambitions.

Kumar Mangalam Birla's elevation to the top position of the Aditya Birla Group at the young age of twenty-eight was necessitated by tragedy—the untimely demise of his legendary father Aditya Vikram Birla. Rising to the challenge of heading what was then India's most globalized homegrown business house, Birla oversaw the growth of the group's turnover from

US$2 billion in 1995 when he took over to more than US$45 billion now. Along the way, he took over Indal, the Indian subsidiary of Alcan, bought large copper mines in Australia, acquired the cement business of L&T, and purchased Novelis, the world's largest producer of aluminium rolled products. The group is truly multinational with a presence in thirty-six countries and 50 per cent of its sales coming from overseas.

Mukesh Ambani became Chairman of Reliance Industries after the death of his father Dhirubhai Ambani. Despite being an inheritor, Ambani set a scorching pace of growth and expanded his petrochemicals- and petroleum products-focused group into telecom, retail, financial services, and new energy. In the process, he has seen his personal net worth grow from about US$2 billion in 2002 to US$92 billion now making him the fifteenth richest person in the world.

All three—Tata, Birla, and Ambani—are inheritors. Yet, all of them are wealth creators without parallel. They attained their iconic status amongst the world's leading wealth creators by showing up, even though they started from a much higher baseline than others.

SHOWING UP NOT LIMITED BY AGE

Did you know: Colonel Harland David Sanders started franchising his secret chicken recipe in 1952, at the age of sixty-two after failing at several professions. Ray Kroc, the founder of the McDonald's fast-food franchise, bought McDonald's from its eponymous owners, in 1961, when he was fifty-nine, after having been a paper cup salesman, a musician, and a milkshake mixer salesperson.

Neither had done much that was remarkable till then. Yet, both went on to found global fast-food franchises that made them multi-millionaires and created billions of dollars of wealth for stakeholders across the world.

These examples prove there is no age limit for showing up. One can do so at any stage of life. Closer home, Ashok Soota, who had worked as a salaried professional all his life, resigned as CEO of Wipro in 1999 to set up Mindtree, an IT services company, which he exited in 2011. That same year, he founded Happiest Minds, an IT services company that offers global clients cloud computing, engineering digital solutions, digital infrastructure, big data analysis, and other managed services. Starting his entrepreneurial journey at the age of fifty-seven, the eighty-one-year-old Soota is a billionaire with a net worth of US$1.1 billion. What could be the motivation for Soota, who is single and has no inheritors for his wealth, to continue on the path of wealth creation at his age? He believes that sky should be the limit for wealth creation since wealth so created could be left behind for the betterment of society.

Readers will note that wealth comes only to those who show up, with age not being a limitation, as the examples of Sanders, Kroc, and Soota show. The Japanese have a term for this: ikigai. It means if you have a larger purpose in life driven by your passion and have the requisite skills to pursue it and if the world needs it too, then society is ready to pay you for it as long as you are at it. It could keep you motivated till the last day of your life, and you will never feel like retiring since you would never be tired.

Thus, wealth comes only to those who show up irrespective of their age or stage in life. One could be a forever wealth creator till the last day of one's life. Wealth creation for such people is life's mission and not just a means to becoming rich.

PART III
LAWS OF MANAGING WEALTH

Chapter 12

WHAT TO DO TO RETAIN WEALTH?

Wealth is accompanied by greed and fear. Both these sentiments could lead to erosion of wealth if not handled well.

Once wealth is created, what does one have to do to safeguard it? Having learnt in the previous section how to create wealth, this section will share nuggets of practical wisdom on retaining wealth, which is as important as creating it. There is no point creating wealth if it does not last. Creating wealth is hard, keeping it once it gets created is even harder. Once you have created wealth, you have something to protect, and you will want more of it. Wealth is accompanied by greed and fear. Both these sentiments could lead to erosion of wealth if not handled well.

DIFFERENCE BETWEEN CREATING AND MANAGING WEALTH

In order to retain wealth, it needs to be managed actively. The management of wealth is very different from its creation. In the journey of creation of wealth, the individual is focused on creating something which he does not own. Once wealth gets created, a big shift happens and the concept of ownership comes into play. Now the individual has something that he owns and with that comes the new responsibility of ownership. It now needs to be looked after and taken care of. That requires a very different mindset and attitude. The resources required to manage the wealth, too, will be very different from those required for creating it.

It is the dream of most Indians to buy their own home. People save money over many years, take loans, and purchase homes for themselves and their families. But buying the house or apartment is not the end of the story. The ownership of the asset brings with it a different set of responsibilities. Bank loans, if any, have to be serviced, maintenance and electricity charges have to be paid regularly, running repairs carried out, the house has to be repainted every few years, and the relevant municipal taxes have to be remitted. These steps are necessary for the upkeep of the property, failing which its value will not appreciate at the desired rate.

In the case of other asset classes like listed equities, the value may even erode over time if the portfolio of listed equity holdings is not managed actively for the simple reason that we live in a dynamic world which is constantly changing the context of various industries and the businesses therein. Therefore, a business that is doing well today may be out of the reckoning a few years down the line and with that its share price will also go down, taking down the wealth of those who own it.

From the previous section we know that the resources required for creating wealth are an idea which solves a problem for the society, adequate financial capital and manpower to take the idea to the market, and the opportunity of a compelling addressable market which will pay for solving the problem. Having become wealthy, the resources required to safeguard the wealth so created will be very different. Managing wealth is a specialized task—as specialized as its creation. While you could use your expertise in your own domain to create wealth, you will need the subject matter expertise of an experienced wealth manager to help you keep your wealth. This individual will have access to relevant and timely information and data, investment opportunities and the necessary tools of the trade that can help you, the wealth owner, to protect and grow your wealth without exposing it to unacceptable levels of risk.

Then, if the quantum of accumulated assets is large, the owner may have to hire managers to take care of the housekeeping—accountants to track tax payments, dividend receipts and rentals, lawyers to look after the paperwork, nominations, renewals and other legal requirements, facilities managers to ensure the upkeep of offices and buildings, and other personnel required for the security and maintenance of the assets.

A shift from wealth creation to wealth ownership requires a shift in the attitude of the wealth owner. Now that there is something to multiply and lose, the sentiments of greed and fear enter the field. One now has the responsibility of ensuring that one's accumulated wealth is not frittered away.

SHIFTING DYNAMICS—FROM WEALTH CREATOR TO WEALTH OWNER

The most important change that comes with the creation of wealth is the sense of responsibility that a corpus of accumulated assets brings with it. Very often, the same person has to simultaneously play both roles. A wealth owner does not stop being a wealth creator after reaching a given threshold of accumulated wealth. While the wealth creation activities continue, the individual also sets aside a part of his/her time and resources towards the active management of the wealth that has been created.

Many wealthy families, therefore, set up trusts and/or family offices to manage their wealth even as they continue to pursue activities that result in the creation of more wealth.

For example, the Tata Trusts have ensured that the massive Tata fortune remains intact, grows, and is used for the good of society while the founder's family retains control of the underlying assets that are managed by professional managers. The founding family of Wipro has set up a large family office to actively manage its wealth, as have the promoters of Bharti Airtel, and several other large business houses.

According to a report in *Inc42*, as on 30 June 2023, there were about 300 family offices in India with average assets under management of US$100 million (₹840 crore). They include several big names such as Piramal, Godrej, DLF, Haldiram's, Mahindra & Mahindra, and Murugappa Group, among others.

The fact that so many ultra-high net worth families are setting up family offices indicates that the management of wealth is a specialized task that is best left to professional wealth managers and advisers. In such cases, while the wealth owner delegates management of the wealth to the wealth advisers under their supervision, they allow themselves the freedom to focus on wealth creation as a perpetual goal. Management of wealth, therefore, requires changes in one's responsibilities, behaviour, and risk appetite.

Responsibility: The most important attitudinal change that has to be inculcated is the altered sense of responsibility. Wealth owners have to always bear in mind the responsibility they carry on their shoulders to ensure the financial security of future generations, especially if the scale of wealth is large enough to go beyond one generation. They become trustees of family legacies and must always remember their duty to ensure the preservation and growth of the wealth in their custody—without exposing it to undue risks.

Behaviour: Owners must also accept that wealth creation and wealth management are two distinct and different functions and require very different behavioural inputs for success. Most wealth creators are hands-on managers but have to learn the art of delegation and letting go when it comes to managing the wealth that they have earned. Since this involves ceding of some control, many wealth creators are unwilling or unable to bring themselves to do it. Additionally, the focus must also change from quarter-on-quarter growth during the wealth creation journey to steady growth and compounding effect over the longer term.

Risks: Individuals typically assume large, albeit calculated risks in their wealth creation journey. Now that the wealth has been created, the appetite for risk has to be aligned with the growth and protection goals that we shall examine in the next chapter. Judicious managers of wealth also look at diversification of wealth to spread the risk of concentration beyond one basket.

WHY MANAGING WEALTH IS IMPORTANT

Let us take a simple example. An individual starts working at the age of twenty-five and saves ₹1 lakh. He invests this in a bank fixed deposit that gives 6 per cent annual interest. At age fifty-five, i.e., after thirty years, he would have earned a total interest of ₹6,000 x 30 = ₹1.8 lakh, giving him a corpus of ₹1 lakh + ₹1.8 lakh = ₹2.8 lakh. To keep this example simple, let us ignore the elements of taxation of returns.

Now, let us assume this individual decided to actively manage his savings and proactively reinvested the interest earned every year in fixed deposits at the same rate of interest. At the end of thirty years, his corpus would have grown to ₹5,74,349. The compounding effect would have more than doubled his savings from the ₹2.8 lakh he would have generated earlier.

Now, what if the individual had hired the services of a professional wealth manager, who invested his savings in instruments that gave returns of 9 per cent per year. In that case, he would have earned returns of ₹12,26,768 over the thirty-year-tenure of the investment and his capital would have grown to ₹13,26,768.

In the example above, the opportunity cost of not managing one's wealth would have been massive—more than ₹10 lakhs. Alternatively, the wealth, if managed would have grown 4.7 times more, to 13.26 lakhs instead of 2.8 lakhs.

Everyone has a finite lifespan, but wealth can remain in a family far beyond the lifetime of the original creator if it is managed properly and systems are in place to ensure its safety and growth. This ensures continuity of wealth in the family even when the founding generation passes the baton on to the next generation. Once the scale of wealth goes beyond one's needs it becomes just a number which will never be used by the wealth owner in his lifetime. In that respect, the wealth owner then becomes the custodian of the wealth in his lifetime which he then leaves behind as his legacy for his future generations. Therefore, active management of wealth by the wealth owner during his lifespan enables him to leave a much larger legacy for his family.

Active management of wealth also does good to the society. Even if a wealth owner makes a deposit with a bank, it does good to the society because the bank lends the money to those needing funds for businesses or other purposes. Likewise, when a wealth owner invests in an equity mutual fund the fund manager uses the same to buy stocks of good quality businesses run by good quality managements which then helps to differentiate a well-run business from poorly managed one. This creates jobs, encourages entrepreneurship, and increases the circle of prosperity by bringing more people within its fold. This brings us back to the lesson we learnt in an earlier section that one person's expense is another person's income. Thus, managing wealth enables social good and helps spread affluence across the society. If, on the other hand, one keeps wealth locked up in a locker, it helps no one and inflation erodes its value over time.

ROLE OF BEHAVIOUR IN RETAINING WEALTH

Many of us must have come across people who have risen from rags to riches. Several such individuals remain strongly grounded even after they have earned large fortunes. Some others, however, lose their humility. Their tone changes and they begin to believe that their wealth has given them a status above their peers. Such people often become arrogant and surround themselves with a coterie of hangers-on who form an echo chamber that only sings the wealth creator's praises. Because of this, they become inaccessible, shut their minds to people and information that could lead to a course correction, and stop receiving new ideas from the world. This obstructs their learning, which triggers the beginning of the end of their wealth creation journey and eventually brings them closer to even losing the wealth that they have created.

Another important behavioural trait that plays an important role in managing and retaining wealth is patience. Nothing of lasting value can ever be created over a short span of time. It is always the result of deep contemplation, good planning, meticulous execution, effective risk mitigation, and efficient management. The common thread that weaves all these into a beautiful tapestry is patience. We have seen in the simple example of investing over thirty years about how compounding can exponentially expand one's wealth—but only if one has the patience to stay the course. The world around us, and especially the economy, is very dynamic and ever changing. It takes immense patience and nerves of steel to be able to weather the ups and downs of life and remain steadfast on the journey of owning, managing, and keeping your wealth or staying rich. There is enough empirical evidence that tells us that being patient is key to retaining and managing one's wealth.

Greed and fear also play a very important role in the management of wealth. The management of wealth involves multiplying it without exposing it to too many risks. So, it is very important for the wealth owner to be aware of both opportunities and risks when they present themselves. However, it is natural for the person to be swayed by both greed—for the opportunity of multiplying the wealth—as well as the fear—for the risk of losing the wealth. It is therefore important to be mindful to avoid falling into the herd mentality trap driven by greed and fear. The stock markets are full of stories of investors who enter the market when it is overheating, attracted by reports of people earning fortunes, only to burn their fingers when the cycle turns. In many such instances, they buy stocks at prices far higher than their intrinsic values and then sell in a panic when the price crashes. Here, we see both greed and fear contributing to the resulting losses, which leads to the erosion of wealth. In contrast, having the patience to stay invested in the market over longer periods of time across market cycles will result in both protection and growth of wealth.

RECIPE FOR MANAGING WEALTH

Similar to the secret formula for creating wealth that we discovered in the earlier section on Laws of Creating Wealth, there is a recipe for managing wealth that we shall learn in this section. These are time-tested rules that help wealth owners preserve the wealth over their lifetime and pass it on as their legacy to their next generation. Some of these are defined by mathematics but most are built on the foundation of self-discipline. Together they create a healthy recipe for managing wealth which can be picked up by every wealth owner. In the following chapters, we shall learn these Laws of Managing Wealth that will allow you to make wealth your lifelong partner.

Chapter 13

PROTECTING AND GROWING

If wealth stops growing, its purchasing power starts diminishing because of inflation. But growing wealth exposes it to the risk of losses. The key, then, lies in finding a balance.

There is an interesting dichotomy between the protection and growth of wealth. Both are important for the sustenance of wealth; yet they are diametrically opposite to each other. If wealth is not growing, then its purchasing power starts diminishing over time on account of inflation. However, if wealth is put on the highway of growth, then it has to encounter the risk of unpredictable accidents and breakdowns. Extremes on either end of the spectrum are not good for the sustenance of wealth. They have to be juggled and balanced to draw the full benefit from their advantages while at the same time tempering their respective downsides. Each of them is a necessary ingredient to the recipe of managing wealth efficiently.

DIFFERENCE BETWEEN PROTECTING AND GROWING WEALTH

Once you have created wealth you have two distinct options to choose from for the future course of managing your wealth—should you protect it or grow it? In the interest of making an informed choice it would be prudent to understand the difference between the two.

There is a wide gulf between protection and growth. They are two distinct goals of managing wealth and sit at the opposite ends of a continuum. The goal of protecting wealth aims to ensure that the principal value of wealth remains intact at all times, whereas the goal of growth of wealth is focussed on increasing the principal value of wealth by allowing it to compound over a period of time. As you can see, the end goals are different in each case. In one case, the reward is the surety of the principal value of wealth at all times; in the case of the other, the reward is the growth in the principal value of wealth over time. While the rewards are different in the two cases, their inherent risks are also different since risk and rewards go hand in hand. In case of the protection goal, the key risk is the erosion in the purchasing power of the wealth over time on account of inflation, while in case of the growth goal, there could be the risk of erosion in the principal value of wealth itself on account of the investment going bad.

Let us see how this works in the real world. Let us take a scenario where you decide to keep your wealth in the form of either cash or in a current account of a bank, which gives you zero return. If the prevailing rate of inflation is 5 per cent, then the basket of goods and services which cost ₹100 today will cost ₹105 one year down the line. This means that the purchasing power of your wealth will come down by roughly 5 per cent and you can afford to buy only 95 per cent of the goods and services one year down the line even though the principal value of your wealth has remained intact at ₹100.

Now, let us move a step forward and assume a scenario where your wealth has grown at the rate of inflation. In this case, you will still be able to buy the same basket of goods and services that you could a year ago. Therefore, you have achieved two goals here—one, you have protected the principal value of your wealth and two, you have protected the purchasing power of your wealth. However, in your quest to keep pace with inflation, you would have taken some investment risk with the principal value of your wealth. Despite this, there has been no improvement in your purchasing power compared to the previous year.

Now, let us move further ahead and assume a scenario where your wealth has grown higher than the rate of inflation, say at 10 per cent when the inflation is 5 per cent. At the end of one year, the principal value of your wealth would have grown to ₹110, which can then buy a bigger basket of goods and services than the earlier basket which is now available at ₹105. In this case, you could achieve the goal of growing the purchasing power of your wealth, which means you have grown your wealth in real terms. However, in your quest to grow your wealth by beating the inflation rate, you would have assumed a higher investment risk, which can expose the principal value of your wealth to the risk of notional erosion on account notional investment losses over the short period of one year. This notional loss could become a real loss if you need the funds and cannot stay invested to recoup the losses over time.

PRIORITISING BETWEEN GROWTH AND PROTECTION

There is no point in creating wealth if you cannot keep it. You must also ensure that the purchasing power of your wealth is not eroding with every passing day. This erosion happens unobtrusively; so, you do not notice it in real time. Realization dawns only when you want to use your wealth to purchase something and find out that it is no longer adequate to cover your proposed acquisition. The examples discussed above show how this works. Therefore, not just the protection of the principal value of the wealth but also the protection of its purchasing power over time is essential to meet the goal of keeping your wealth in the real sense.

At the same time, growth is equally important as it helps to increase the purchasing power of your wealth as explained in the third scenario above. If your wealth and its purchasing power do not grow, you will not be able to afford to upgrade your lifestyle. When you protect your wealth, you certainly protect your current lifestyle. However, it also means that you have reached the saturation level of your lifestyle for the rest of your life. The concept of pension illustrates this example very well. A pension scheme is income generated during one's retirement years on the corpus saved over the working/earning years of that individual. The retirement corpus is finite and cannot be increased once one has stopped earning, since contributions to that corpus stop at the time of the retirement. Accordingly, any income on that, too, shall be finite and may only have inflation adjusted revisions with time. This would protect the pensioner's existing lifestyle but will not leave any room for upgrading it over rest of his/her life. On the contrary, if you have both the willingness as well as the ability to assume higher investment risk after income protection goals have been taken care of, then still not growing the wealth will lead to the opportunity cost of missing out on compounding your wealth over time.

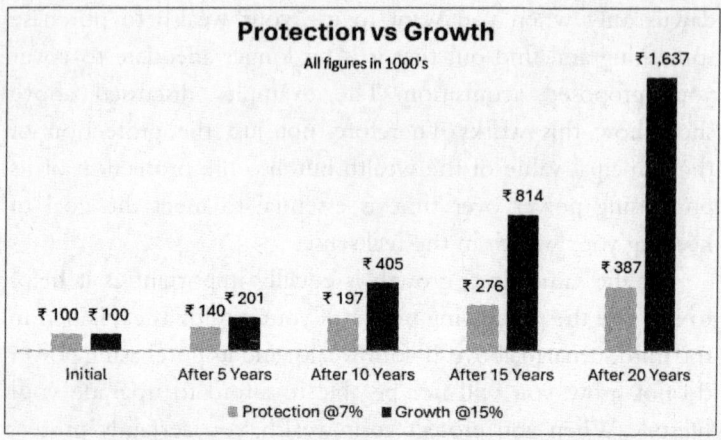

Image 12: Difference between protection and growth of wealth

Having understood the importance of growing your wealth, it must also be appreciated that higher risk comes with the potential for higher returns. Therefore, an individual has to seek a fine balance between the two competing goals of protection and growth of wealth. We will understand later in this chapter how to arrive at this balance.

Therefore, growth is as important as protection—but only after you have secured your basic needs with low-risk investments. You can then utilize your surplus savings for growth purposes. Obviously, there cannot be a one size fits all formula to the protection versus growth question. The answer will depend on your ability to take risk and grow your wealth. This will be defined by your lifestyle, life stage, needs, and the scale of wealth already created. It also depends on your willingness to take risks even though you may have the ability to take such risks.

In the context of somebody who has already created wealth, the thumb rule should be to secure yourself first and only then look for opportunities to grow your wealth.

RISKS AND REWARDS

We have seen in the examples above that not growing your wealth or an excessive focus only on the protection of the principal will lead to eroding your purchasing power owing to inflation. If you have ₹100 and this amount remains constant over a long period of time, you actually suffer an erosion of wealth because of lower purchasing power. But if you focus solely on maintaining your purchasing power, then you have no scope to upgrade your lifestyle, which is a legitimate and desirable aspiration.

Your peers, friends, and extended family might have upgraded their lifestyles with the passage of time. When phones, cars, and other gadgets become old, people upgrade to newer models. As incomes rise, people buy larger homes, spend on more lavish holidays, and improve the quality of their lives. For example, only a handful of people in India owned cars half a century ago. Now, millions of people do. Mobile phones did not exist in India till as recently as a quarter of a century ago. Now, they are ubiquitous. Eating out was not very common before the 1990s. Thanks to rising purchasing power, it is no longer considered a luxury. All these point to the fact that society is forever upgrading to a higher quality of living. If your financial planning only takes care of your current levels of sustenance, you will never be able to upgrade and, consequently, will be left behind by the tide of time. There is, therefore, the risk that your purchasing power will remain constant or, in a worst-case scenario, even go down to a level where you can no longer afford things you could in earlier times.

We have seen in a previous chapter that wealth creates

wealth. The multiplier effect of compounding will grow your wealth exponentially even while you sleep. So, when you are focused only on protection, you not only miss out on growth but the compounding effect on the growth as well.

OPPORTUNITIES FOR PROTECTING AND GROWING WEALTH

A soldier wearing a bulletproof jacket feels safer taking on the enemy in the defence of his/her motherland because of the knowledge that he/she is secure from enemy fire. This assurance of safety enables him/her to fight better. Likewise, one would be ready to jump into the ocean from a ship if one is wearing a life jacket. Similarly, once you've been vaccinated for yellow fever you will be confident to go on a Kenyan safari. Expeditions to Antarctica have been undertaken with the teams camping on the icy continent for months on the assurance of adequate supplies of food and fuel in their backyard to keep them alive.

Much like these examples, when you know that you are financially secure, both your ability and willingness to take risks will rise in tandem. Let us understand this with the help of a simple case. Say, your total wealth is ₹200, out of which you need ₹100 to protect your financial freedom. Once you are able to put the first ₹100 on the job to earn adequate income to secure your lifestyle and life goals, it frees the remaining 50 per cent of your wealth to be put on the highway of growth. You know that you are unlikely to need the surplus wealth for a very long time, maybe even in your entire lifetime, and, therefore, you could put that to compound over the rest of your life. Your ability to take risks with your surplus wealth will be much higher since you know that are not dependent on it for your financial security. When you know that you have the ability to take greater risks, your willingness to take greater risks and face more uncertainty also goes up, which then leads to growth. Protection of wealth as the first goal then becomes the foundation for the growth of wealth. This enabling cause-and-effect relationship between protection and growth applies to an individual, a family, a business, or even a country.

That is how successful entrepreneurs such as Elon Musk, Mukesh Ambani, and Ratan Tata have expanded their businesses into multibillion-dollar global conglomerates. Since their companies have strong balance sheets, their ability to take risks is correspondingly higher, which gives confidence to bankers and investors to pour billions of dollars into their expansion programs. This helps to fuel their continuous growth.

Let us take the example of the Indian banking sector. A decade ago, Indian banks were weighed down by the burden of unpaid loans—known as non-performing assets (NPAs) in banking language. This severely restricted their ability to advance fresh loans to new borrowers. Many borrowers, too, were stuck with large loans that they could not service. This impacted their credit profiles and severely impaired their ability to expand. However, concerted efforts by the government, bank managements, and the Reserve Bank of India have brought the situation back under control. The NPA position of Indian banks is now relatively more benign compared to what it was a few years ago. As a result of being protected, Indian banks are once again both able and willing to lend growth capital to Indian industry, which has significantly contributed at the macro level to India's GDP, which recorded a growth of 8.2 per cent in 2023-24 (as per the National Statistics Office).

While protection has an enabling relationship with growth it could be the other way around if growth is given precedence over protection. It is similar to having bravado instead of prudence. In such a scenario, one's risk appetite not only remains intact but could even go up, emboldened by positive outcomes as the wealth is growing well with the underlying risks that have been assumed.

However, when the cycle turns and the outcomes start going downhill, it results in a cascading impact on the risk appetite, since there is no downside protection. This often results in the flight of capital from risk to safety on account of a dramatic aversion to risk. In this process, if some part of the wealth has been lost, it could leave permanent scars on the risk appetite of the wealth owner.

When this happens, it creates a long-term adverse impact on the growth of wealth and, given the adverse experience, one may not be prepared to take the risk of any further pain. We see this play out in various real-life situations in the world we live in.

A start-up that focuses only on growth at any cost becomes dependent on external capital to keep funding its losses and remain alive. It is able to remain in the game only till such time that it is able to raise the next round of equity funding. However, the moment it loses the confidence of investors, it finds itself in a situation where there is no one to bail it out and is eventually forced to shutter its operations. Every start-up cannot be an Amazon and every start up founder cannot be Jeff Bezos who could convince his stakeholders that Amazon would be hugely profitable one day at the scale of revenues that Amazon has now.

BALANCING GROWTH AND PROTECTION GOALS

As we have seen, both growth and protection are important goals and so, it is critical to juggle between the two. An individual who has already created wealth must learn to strike a balance based specifically on his/her own circumstances and needs. Here, one must be clear about what is a need and what constitutes a want. The former is something without which your life would be incomplete. The latter is something that could add value to your existence but the absence of which will not have a debilitating impact on you. While wants are nice to have things in life, needs are defined by must have things in life. Needs would essentially include key life goals like retirement planning, lifestyle protection, education of kids, healthcare goals, and family and social events like milestone celebrations and weddings. This interplay between needs and wants is dynamic and keeps evolving over time, as a function of what we can afford, as well as the improvements and developments in technology. Therefore, one needs to have a dynamic approach towards financial planning to remain in sync with the needs of the times.

Once needs have been understood well, they will have to be quantified in terms of the quantum of wealth that will be required to fund them. When balancing between protection and the growth of wealth, one's needs will have to be prioritized. Arrangements will have to be made to protect this baseline. Any wealth that is available beyond this baseline amount can then be allocated towards the growth goal.

This equation between protection and growth goals can never be the same for two individuals since everyone's situation is unique on account of various factors like the scale of wealth, lifestyle, life stage, and life goals. One individual may have a lavish lifestyle that requires a large scale of wealth to fund. Another may have a modest standard of living requiring a much smaller scale of wealth to sustain. However, the ability of the more affluent individual to take risks could be relatively higher. This could result in a higher allocation towards the growth goal as compared to protection even though he/she will need a much higher amount of wealth in absolute terms to secure his/her needs.

So, every individual must first assess their needs based on their own unique circumstances and then take a call on how to proceed. But the thumb rule will remain the same, irrespective of a person's financial standing or social status: first protect your needs and only then focus on growth. We shall examine the interplay between needs and wants in the next chapter.

Chapter 14

EXPENSES AND LIFESTYLE MANAGEMENT

Lifestyle inflation is a bigger threat to wealth erosion than financial inflation. Therefore, lifestyle management becomes a critical component of wealth management.

An important aspect of keeping the wealth is respecting it. Just as wealth does not come to you without you having a desire for it, it may not stay with you for very long if you do not treat it with respect. In day-to-day life, this gets reflected in how you use your wealth as the currency for funding your cost of living. In India, it is common for parents to teach their children to cut their coat according to their cloth. Simply, if the cost of your lifestyle is more than your resources, it is the surest path to wiping out your wealth. This is applicable in business as well. If the business is incurring losses and capital is funding the deficit, then the capital will get wiped out one day. Lifestyle inflation is a bigger threat to wealth erosion than financial inflation. It is important to understand the fine difference between needs and wants. Therefore, lifestyle management becomes a critical component of wealth management.

UNDERSTANDING THE PROFIT EQUATION

Let us begin with understanding the interplay between wealth, income, and expenses based on an equation that was as relevant 2,000 years back as it is today. This is an equation that everyone instinctively knows: Profit = Income–Expenses. As per this equation, profit is nothing else but excess of income after expenses. While this is applicable for business it is equally applicable when it comes to an individual where the profits become savings and the equation. Then it can be better understood as Savings = Income-Lifestyle Expenses. If savings are accumulated and invested it leads to the creation of wealth over a period of time. Now let us examine the application of this equation in real-life situations.

Let us take a scenario where one is still active in professional life or business and has a steady stream of income. There could be two situations here—one, where the lifestyle expenses are less than the income and two, where they are higher than the income. In the first case, the individual is able to save and add to his wealth built through accumulated savings over the years. Moreover, he doesn't need to dip into his savings to fund his lifestyle expenses and therefore his wealth is able to continue to compound and grow. Accordingly, this person is able to continue to grow his wealth.

In the second case, the lifestyle expenses of the person are higher than his current income. Therefore, he would need to dip into his wealth built over the years to fund the deficit between his income and lifestyle expenses. Not only does this person start eating into his capital or wealth, he has to also set aside an adequate portion of his wealth in liquid assets yielding low or negligible returns which can be drawn on a recurring basis to fund his recurring deficit. This means that he can't afford to put his entire wealth to compound over the longer term. The combined effect of dipping into his capital and his overall wealth compounding at a lower rate will lead to this person's wealth declining in absolute terms and could be lost forever if his lifestyle expenses remain higher than his income over a long period of time.

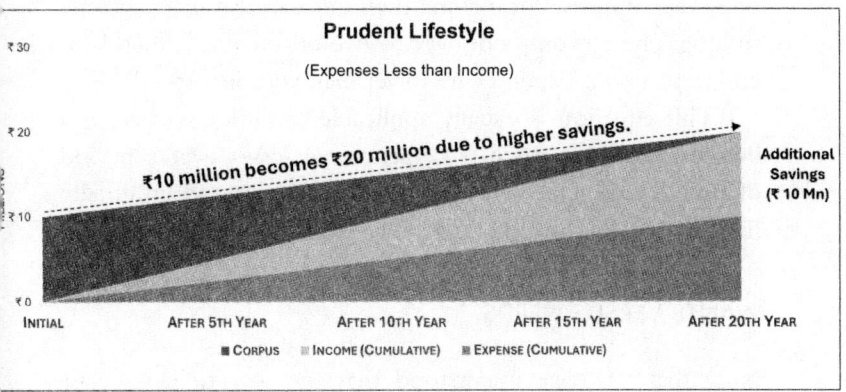

Image 13: When lifestyle expenses are less than income the corpus grows

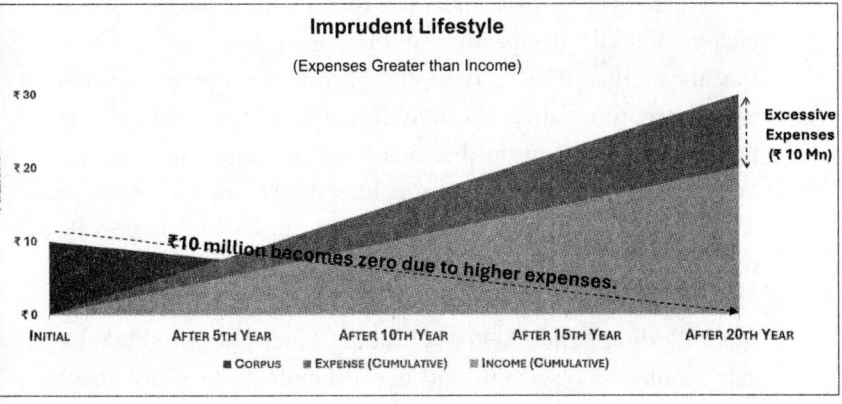

Image 14: When lifestyle expenses are higher than income the corpus reduces

This situation is applicable to even someone who has retired where the source of income now is that generated by the wealth accumulated by this person over his working years. Even in this case if the lifestyle expenses are higher than the income that he is able to generate, he'll end up consuming his wealth eventually. The moral of the story is that if one lives off one's capital instead of income then one's wealth shall last only so long. There is only one way to live off income, which is to ensure that your expenses are lower than your income.

This equation is equally applicable to business where if a business continues to make operational losses over a period of time it will end up eating into its reserves and eventually have to file for bankruptcy.

WANTS VERSUS NEEDS

Now that we have understood that the way to keep your wealth is by managing your lifestyle expenses let's examine if there is a way to regulate them.

We have seen that lifestyle expenses shouldn't overshoot current income irrespective of the sources of income. Does this mean that if over time the income of the person has grown ten times then his lifestyle expenses too could go up ten times? Does it mean that there can be a linear relationship between growth in income and lifestyle expenses over time? The answer to this is a clear 'No' and can be understood by the concept of needs and wants.

Needs are requirements of life. The most basic ones are food, clothing, and shelter. Without these, one wouldn't be able to survive, be secure, and live a dignified life. Once these are taken care of come the next level needs of education, healthcare, and mobility. While the needs remain the same for all individuals there would always be a difference of the threshold of addressing them as a function of the scale of wealth and income of an individual. For example, an affluent person may consume premium food items, buy expensive clothes and accessories, live in a bigger home in an affluent neighbourhood, send his children overseas for education, access private healthcare facilities, and drive a luxury car. However, consumption needs of every individual are finite in terms of quantity. As the scale of your income and wealth rises, an upgrade in lifestyle is bound to happen but it needn't be in proportion to the growth in income. Keeping the expenditure lower means that one will be able to save more with the rise in income and accumulate more wealth earlier.

Wants on the other hand are limitless. They are nice to have things in life as compared to needs which are must to have. While food is a basic necessity for survival and one has only a finite appetite for consumption, one may want to have his daily meals in ware made of gold. Likewise, one can have an endless collection of clothes and accessories and could want to own a home in every part of the world. Wants could be forever limitless and they keep igniting the next threshold of wants. They can keep going up not just in tandem with the growth of income but could grow faster than the growth in income as well.

If you are driven by needs your lifestyle expenses will always be less than your income allowing you to not only keep your wealth but grow it too. On contrary, if you are driven by wants then your lifestyle expenses will always be higher than of your income, putting you at the risk of eventually eating into your wealth.

So, even if your income rises tenfold but your expenses go up fifteenfold you'll eventually end up consuming your entire wealth. This is a trap that many new wealth creators fall into. They feel that with the rise in their wealth they can buy anything. A Google search of lottery winners who lost it all will throw up dozens of examples of people from all over the world who won multimillion-dollar lotteries only to lose all their wealth over the next few years. On the other hand, you will also come across dozens of stories of billionaires who continue to live relatively frugal lives despite being super wealthy. Legendary investor Warren Buffett lives in the relatively modest home he bought back in 1958 for $31,500 in Omaha and still drives his own car that he bought nine years ago. Wipro Chairman Emeritus Azim Premji leads a famously frugal lifestyle. He shuns luxury cars and an ostentatious lifestyle. Other Indian industrialists such as Ratan Tata and Narayana Murthy too lead frugal lives relative to the scale of their wealth.

Any one of the above men could own islands, palaces, and yachts if they wanted to. But as the saying goes, owning an island is a want, while living in a comfortable home is a need.

Just as a competent farmer will not over harvest his land that gives him a healthy crop every year, a prudent wealth creator will take care to lead a financially disciplined life in order to keep the wealth which has been earned over a lifetime. Unless you respect the wealth, it will leave you.

LIMITING LIFESTYLE EXPENSES

Any individual's consumption needs are finite. How much can one eat, drink, and wear? If one is driven by this fact then one will never go overboard. However, every now and then, there are reports of a celebrity splurging on fifty pairs of shoes or thirty handbags or hundreds of suits and saris. They make news and become the talk of the town for days and months.

Former first lady of the Philippines Imelda Marcos became notorious around the world for having a collection of thousands of shoes and bags and hundreds of gowns and other accessories that she may or may not have ever used.

Some people, however, cannot seem to resist the urge to splurge. One does not really need fifty pairs of shoes or thirty bags to live. Such people have to realize that lifestyle expenses cannot and should not be driven by wants. The principal of needs being finite should define one's limit. Readers should keep in mind, however, that there will never be a one size fits all formula to gauge needs and wants. Different people will have different standards and requirements. For example, Person A may be satisfied with two or three pairs of shoes and a similar number of suits, whereas Person B might think he needs twelve of each. But even the most extravagant individual will have to accept that owning fifty items of each is transgressing the limits of need by a wide margin.

Readers should also always remember that when the scale of wealth is small, the percentage of expenses will be higher. That is because one has to incur certain minimum expenses as a fixed cost of living. For example, rental or EMI for the house that one is living in, society maintenance charges, utility charges, expenses on commuting, and cost of basic food and clothing have to be provided for.

At lower levels of income, these will account for a higher percentage of your earnings. As your earning grows, this expenditure should gradually come down in percentage terms. For example, if you earn ₹100 today and your expenses are ₹80, chances are that when your income rises to ₹500, your expenses will rise but by a smaller percentage to, say

₹200. In this example, you were earlier spending 80 per cent of your income, but now are spending only 40 per cent. If your expenses do not fall as a percentage of your income, then that is a cause for concern. It means lifestyle inflation has started eating into your capacity to save, thus, hampering your ability to create wealth.

Once again, the key criteria to watch out for is: are you driven by needs or wants? If it is the former, then you are on track to create more wealth, and more importantly safeguard your exiting wealth from getting consumed. If it is the latter, then you could be on a one-way journey to erosion of wealth. It is time to take stock of your lifestyle and expenses, clearly define your needs and wants and then decide which expenses to continue with and which ones to pare down.

LIFESTYLE INFLATION: THE SINGLE BIGGEST THREAT TO KEEPING YOUR WEALTH

Two recent examples of celebrity multi-millionaires who frittered away their fortunes by leading extravagant lifestyles that were beyond their means are boxer Mike Tyson and tennis legend Boris Becker.

According to a report in the *New York Times*, Tyson, who had a fortune of $300 million, blew up his wealth on a lifestyle without any limits. The report says he spent $400,000 a month on himself, $410,000 on a birthday party, and $65,000 on hiring limousines wherever he travelled. Such a lifestyle was beyond the capacity of even someone as wealthy as Tyson. By 2003, when he was thirty-seven, he was bankrupt with debts of over $27 million.

Tennis legend Boris Becker, who became the youngest Wimbledon champion in 1985 when he was only seventeen, went on to win six Grand Slams and was the No. 1 ranked player in the world for some time. During his playing days, he earned an estimated fortune of $185 million. But a spendthrift habit and a jet-set lifestyle spelt financial doom for this one-time tennis wunderkind.

A report in *Fox Sports* quoted him saying in the Apple TV+ documentary *Boom! Boom! The World versus Boris Becker*: 'We assume the money we earn during our careers will continue to come in afterwards. So, we don't adapt our lifestyles quickly enough. You keep spending money you don't make any more, you keep spending money that you made before. So, yeah, I'm blaming me.'

That statement sums up in a nutshell the essence of this chapter—that it is prudent to assume that the inflow of money will stop in the future and so, it is necessary to adapt one's lifestyle to that reality. Not doing so can lead to the downfall of even ultra-wealthy individuals.

Every wealth owner has to be mindful of both financial inflation as well as lifestyle inflation. Lifestyle inflation can easily be measured by arriving at the increase in your lifestyle expenses one year down the line less prevailing financial inflation. Mathematically, if financial inflation is 5 per cent and lifestyle inflation is 10 per cent then you need to grow your income at the rate of 15 per cent every year just to retain the purchasing power of wealth to meet the demands of the lifestyle which is constantly getting upgraded. Keeping pace with financial inflation is hard, doing the same with lifestyle inflation is much harder. If you are upgrading your lifestyle faster than the growth of your income, then at some point you will need to start dipping into your accumulated wealth, which eventually will get eroded.

Lifestyle inflation is considered a bigger threat to wealth

retention than financial inflation because the latter is usually cyclical in nature. In any dynamic economy, the rate of inflation will spike in some years and then turn moderate or even benign sometime later. Lifestyle inflation is a lot more difficult, if not impossible, to wind down. For example, if you live in a large apartment in a high-end neighbourhood, it will be difficult to adjust to life in a smaller apartment in a less desirable location. If you have got used to being driven around in a luxury car, it will be very difficult to downgrade to a mid-range car that you might have to drive yourself.

That's why, as Boris Becker did, most people find it impossible to adjust to situations where they have to downgrade their lifestyles. Not being able to adapt leads to loss of capital, which is nothing else but wealth erosion. Therefore, to safeguard your hard-earned wealth over your lifetime your lifestyle has to be driven by your needs and not wants.

THE IMPORTANCE OF LIFESTYLE MANAGEMENT

Lifestyle management is a critical component of managing wealth. It is not how much you earn that determines your level of affluence over a period of time but how you lead your life—your habits, needs, and wants. Learning to discipline one's desires and keeping the impulse of spending in check is, therefore, of critical importance for wealth retention.

Upgrading your lifestyle by graduating to more expensive products, bigger homes in more desirable neighbourhoods, bigger luxury cars, and flying first class, among others, are examples of lifestyle inflation. Expending your money on all these items is fine so long as you are living within your means, or, in other words, your income is greater than your expenses. If that is not the case, then, you will be eroding your wealth.

One must always bear in mind that a healthy bank balance or a hefty pay cheque hitting your bank account every month is no indicator of affluence. What lies in your bank account is money and not wealth. It represents your short-term liquidity which is usually only a small part of your overall wealth built over a longer period of time. Your bank balance could be sufficient to meet your immediate lifestyle expenses but it will not be funding your life goals for which you need the reserves of your wealth. However, if you have been progressively dipping into your wealth to fund your ever-growing lifestyle it won't be left to meet your life goals. Thus, lifestyle inflation can be more dangerous than financial inflation and needs to be guarded against at all times.

Chapter 15

EGO VERSUS SELF-RESPECT

Self-management is the bedrock of wealth management. If wealth becomes the fuel for one's ego, it will lead to its destruction. Following the tenets of financial and lifestyle discipline are critical to the art of retaining wealth.

Every human craves respect. There are two sources of respect—external and internal. When it is external, it is called ego; and when it is internal, we call it self-respect. The word self-respect implies that we know our worth and are not dependent on any external gratification. If it is the ego that drives wealth creation, eventually, the wealth will be destroyed. If our decisions are driven by the desire to attract external attention, then the outcomes will invariably be poor. In the context of wealth, such decisions will lead to allocation of wealth towards inefficient goals, which may then lead to erosion of wealth. We may make aggressive investment decisions to impress our peer group. We may make business decisions which may look bold but could result in poor return on capital. We may take lifestyle decisions that could lead to erosion of wealth.

That is the reason experts say self-management is the bedrock of wealth management. Unless you learn to manage yourself well and follow the tenets of financial and lifestyle discipline, it will be difficult to retain the wealth you have created. Once you have created wealth, you should ask yourself the following questions: What must I do to be able to retain it? How should I guard against its erosion? What habits must I cultivate to ensure that I can remain affluent?

WHY WE SEEK RECOGNITION

Awards and recognitions serve a deeply felt emotional need of human beings. Every individual craves the respect and admiration of his peers and fellow beings in society. This is a natural phenomenon and exists in all societies—whether capitalist, communist, theocratic, or dictatorship. To address this urge of human beings to gain recognition, an entire ecosystem of awards industry has developed around the world. These awards have acquired the status of popular platforms so much so that they turn their winners into celebrities. Like any other business, they too are solving a unique problem for society— the need for recognition. Then, there is a case of awards and recognitions coming from institutions and governments that bestow individuals and organizations with institutional/state honours.

The most coveted award in the world is the Nobel Prize. Every year, an individual or group of individuals who have excelled in their chosen field of activity are awarded the Nobel Prize for Literature, Physics, Chemistry, Medicine, Economics, and Peace. The awardees gain instant fame across the world that raises their profiles and prestige for the rest of their lives.

In the entertainment world, every year, people all over the world look forward to the Oscars and Grammys awards ceremonies. Weeks before the events, media houses across the world run commentaries and analyses on the likely winners of these coveted awards. The winners gain renewed validation of their star status and immense prestige and respect from their peers and strangers alike. Then, dozens of English, West Indian, Australian, and New Zealand cricketers, such as Don Bradman, Gary Sobers, Geoffrey Boycott, and Richard Hadlee have been honoured with knighthoods—the title of Sir—for their achievements in the game.

Closer home, the government confers the Padma awards on people who have achievements of note. Sports and film stars also are also bestowed with awards like the Arjuna Award and National Film Award for their excellence in their chosen field. Likewise, there are prestigious awards for almost every field of human activity—for excellence in literature, science, business, social service, etc.

That the need for recognition is deeply ingrained in the human psyche will be evident from the fact that even children have the urge to be recognized. An individual's first brush with the feel-good factor that comes with recognition is when, as a child, he/she receives praise and a pat on the back from family elders for something well done. This continues into school when class toppers are feted before the school assembly and those excelling in sports, debates, quizzing, and other extra-curricular activities are similarly rewarded for excelling in their chosen field.

Look at your own peer group. Can you identify even one individual who will be unhappy at the prospect of winning an award or a public recognition of some sort—from his/her employer, peer group, industry association, or government?

DIFFERENT SOURCES OF RECOGNITION AND THEIR IMPACT ON OUR SELF-WORTH

Human beings constantly seek recognition as validation for their self-esteem. It is important for us to be assured about ourselves and the journey of life that we are on. Recognition in any form reassures us that we are on the right path and that we are progressing well. We have discussed the external sources of recognition in the previous section. The internal source of recognition lies with the self. It implies that we know ourselves well and are aware of our own self-worth. We know as much of our strengths as we do of our weaknesses. We know what we can do as well as what we cannot. It means that we have complete clarity about who we are and the larger purpose of our life. When this happens, it means that we are anchored from within, are self-assured and, therefore, are not dependent on any external source for the validation of who we are or what should be our life's journey.

At this point, let us examine the impact of internal and external sources of recognition in our lives with the help of a few real-life examples around us. A petrol motor car will run only as long as it has fuel in its tank. A smartphone will work only as long its battery has life. There are two things that are common in these examples—one, their source of energy is external and two, they are active as long as that energy pool is not extinguished. Likewise, an individual whose source of validation is external will need a constant supply of external validation to remain self-assured, confident, and happy. In the absence of the same, he/she could be plagued by self-doubt which may start depleting his/her self-esteem. Such people are constantly seeking recognition from external sources. When they get it, they remain motivated, and life feels good; when they do not, they feel depressed. In a way their own life is beyond their control.

However, people whose source of recognition is internal to them are self-assured and have the confidence to carry on with their mission in life regardless of whether their efforts are being recognized and rewarded or not. They are driven by the hunger to go about their tasks based on their inner conviction and belief in themselves. Since they are not driven by the output, they are less fearful of the outcomes and, therefore, are able to take more risks in life. They know what they are doing, why they are doing it, and where they are headed. Even failures do not deter them.

Failures become the stepping stones to success for self-assured and confident people. They learn the right lessons from their failures and use that knowledge to blaze a trail that leads to success. They keep learning along the way as failures teach them what not to do and success shows them what they need to do more of. They are truly masters of their life, karma yogis.

DIFFERENCE BETWEEN EGO AND SELF-RESPECT

Now that we have seen how every individual has the need for recognition and that the source of recognition is different for everyone, let us see how this manifests differently in our behaviour.

When an individual is driven by ego, he/she acts so as to attract the attention of third parties, even when rationality demands a less flamboyant course of action. In other words, ego is the visible manifestation of somebody whose source of recognition is external to that person. On the contrary, humility is the visible manifestation of someone's behaviour whose source of recognition is internal to that person based on self-respect.

In real-life situation, this will find expression in the way an individual behaves with peers and other members of society. The way this individual engages with people will make it evident whether he/she is driven by ego or self-respect. An individual driven by ego will be very conscious of his/her position. Such a person expects others to go to him; he/she will never go to other people. He/she will expect his/her neighbours and peers to wish him/her first and only then return their greetings. They feel happy when others wish them because they take this as a sign of their own exalted status in society. Conversely, they are upset when others do not greet them first and see such behaviour as disrespectful. This kind of behaviour is not limited to the public sphere alone. We often witness this kind of behaviour within families, among friends, between parents and grown-up children, and also between siblings.

It is also quite common in the sports field. In team sports, some senior players who have been in the team for a while expect juniors to defer to them and show respect.

In his autobiography *Imperfect*, former cricketer and noted commentator Sanjay Manjrekar wrote that the atmosphere in the team in the early-1990s was unpleasant. Among the reasons he has cited was the attitude of some unnamed seniors who expected newcomers to treat them with respect. At team meetings, in the team manager's hotel room, the seniors would occupy the chairs and even sprawl on sofas and the bed while the newcomers would have to sit on the floor. Given this disturbed atmosphere in the team, it should come as no surprise that the performance of the Indian cricket team in that era was middling.

On the other hand, people driven by self-respect, as we have seen above, are highly self-assured and confident in their own skin. Their behaviour, in most cases, is the polar opposite of the conduct described in the foregoing paragraphs.

Individuals in leadership positions like CEOs in the corporate world and captains in the world of sports who are not driven by their egos are more open to critical feedback, which helps them to keep their ear to the ground and take decisions which are aligned with ground realities. There is a higher probability that such decisions will lead to success.

On the other hand, individuals in leadership positions who are driven by ego are extremely conscious of how they are perceived by their followers. They are usually less open to feedback, especially if it is not in alignment with their own thinking. Therefore, they try to insulate themselves from any opposition by surrounding themselves with yes men. Accordingly, the decisions taken by them may be out of sync with ground realities and, more often than not, prone to unfavourable outcomes. This will have a diametrically opposite impact on the net worth of these two individuals. A leader who is driven by self-respect has a higher probability of succeeding. This will have a positive effect on the creation and growth of wealth for the ecosystem around that individual, his/her immediate stakeholders as well for himself/herself. It will be the reverse for the leader driven by ego. Accordingly, it can be concluded that the relationship between self-worth and net worth is directly proportional. The higher the self-worth, the higher will be the probability of higher net worth. Self-respect is the bridge to keeping your wealth.

RELATIONSHIP OF EGO AND SELF-RESPECT WITH WEALTH IN PERSONAL AND PROFESSIONAL SITUATIONS

We've seen the correlation between input and output and hunger and greed in earlier chapters. Ego and self-respect share a similar relationship. Ego makes an individual focus on output rather than input. It makes one do things that are designed to attract attention even if such a course of action is not the most prudent in the given circumstances.

For example, readers will be familiar with examples of business tycoons who expanded into unrelated lines of business, not necessarily to grow the business, earn more money or benefit society, but to gain validation and appreciation and earn the applause of the media and their social circuit. The ill-fated expansion programmes were vehicles to show off one's wealth and earn brownie points. These were examples of grandstanding rather than prudent and financially rational decisions. Since the tycoons concerned were investing money in pursuit of applause, and economic returns were not the primary driver of their decisions, the expansion programmes did not pan out as envisaged and led to the erosion of wealth not only for the business leaders involved but also for other stakeholders like lender banks, suppliers and vendors, employees, and customers.

On the other hand, business houses like the Tatas, Reliance, Aditya Birla and others that also embarked on ambitious expansion programs succeeded in adding value and creating more wealth because their plans were based on solid foundations of detailed planning and meticulous execution guided by business fundamentals.

In a team sport like cricket, a self-assured and confident player will not mind batting at a position that is best for the team. A hard-hitting middle order batsman might be needed to open the innings if the team needs quick runs at the top when chasing victory in a limited time period. A defensive opening batsman, on the other hand, may be asked by the team management to bat lower down the order as insurance against a top order collapse while the team chases quick runs in pursuit of victory.

A self-assured player who puts his/her team above his/her own interests and performs, gains the respect of his/her peers, fans, and other stakeholders. If they can do this over a long period of time, they become indispensable to the team. This attitude earns him/her the respect and admiration of the public at large and results in greater potential for wealth creation via a longer playing career, higher match fees, and more endorsements.

We see the limiting effect of ego in organizations that get trapped in peer comparisons. Very often, we compare two individuals, two companies, or two countries. The point of this comparison is to do better than the rival. So, even if one company has the potential to do twice as well as the rival, the act of benchmarking itself to its rival might restrict it from reaching its full potential.

In family situations, we come across cases of families that have broken up because of ego problems between its members—partners, siblings, and also between parents and children. When families go through separation, their members do get their personal independence but at the same time, also have to incur the cost of separation in terms of family settlements based on a division of family wealth and assets. To achieve this, the family has to pull out its wealth from avenues where it may be getting compounded to divide and distribute amongst its warring stakeholders. This invariably leads to erosion of wealth for the family as a whole.

On the other hand, we also come across cases of families that are driven by the values of mutual respect, caring, and sharing. Such families respect, recognize, and celebrate each of its members as they are leaving no room for comparisons and rivalry. Anecdotal evidence suggests that such families are usually more successful in creating, safeguarding, growing, and retaining their wealth.

Moving on from family to individual situation, the interplay between ego, self-respect, and wealth is equally visible. For an individual driven by ego the source of recognition is external which could manifest in lifestyle decisions. One may choose to take lifestyle decisions driven by the desire for seeking external validation rather than need. One may decide to move to a mansion from a comfortable home or move to an upmarket address to be seen and counted as having arrived in life. One may decide to acquire a fleet of expensive cars and travel first class. None of these decisions may pass the test of financial prudence and could be drain on your wealth as we have examined in the earlier chapter on Expenses and Lifestyle Management. Some of these assets so acquired could be depreciating in nature as we shall examine in the following chapter. On the contrary, individuals who are driven by self-respect have no such urge to seek external validation and therefore are able to safeguard, grow, and keep their wealth.

SELF-MANAGEMENT IS CRITICAL FOR MANAGING OUR WEALTH

We have learnt in Chapter 14 the importance of lifestyle management in safeguarding wealth. We have seen when wealth is allocated towards wants instead of needs it will erode our wealth. Our wants are driven by our ego and are fed by the need for external validation. This makes self-management important for retaining wealth. Individuals who are able to manage themselves better than others are also able to regulate their lifestyle expenses. In that context, self-management is rather more critical than lifestyle management in managing your wealth. Not winning an Oscar does not make an actor inferior to another actor who has won the coveted award. An individual who is driven by self-respect is anchored from within and is well aware that awards and recognitions are the by-products of excellence. Such an individual will not chase awards as the end goal of the journey and, therefore, will not need to fritter away his/her time, resources, and wealth to seek adulation.

Individuals with self-assurance and awareness of self-worth usually have greater reserves of humility than those driven by ego because humility is nothing but knowing oneself and others around oneself. People with humility know what they can do as well as what is beyond them. Likewise, they are also able to accept those around them the way they are. Humility, therefore, helps people to remain grounded and closer to reality. It enables people to play to their own strengths rather than compare and compete with one's rivals. And when people play their own game based on their strengths, the probability of success is higher.

We can relate this to a real-life example of auctions. Most people have heard the term 'winner's curse'. We see this at play in auctions, which begin with inviting bids over a reserve price. Bidding by design is a competitive process where bidders have to bid higher and higher to win the right to buy a given asset. A competitive bidding process can push bidders to bid much higher than the intrinsic value of the asset being auctioned. Now, for a bidder driven by ego, winning the bid will become a matter of prestige even though it may not make economic sense. On the other hand, a bidder driven by self-respect will have the humility and prudence to accept the futility of winning the asset at an inflated price and, therefore, will know when to stop bidding and withdraw from the auction. In the first case, the winner of the auction will find it hard to keep his wealth, whereas the one who withdraws from the irrational race will be able to keep his wealth. Therefore, behaviour driven by ego invariably leads to erosion of wealth whereas actions driven by self-respect enable one to protect, grow, and keep wealth. Therefore, self-management is the bedrock of wealth management.

Chapter 16

DEPRECIATING VERSUS APPRECIATING ASSETS

To protect and grow your wealth you should invest in appreciating assets. Spending your wealth on depreciating assets should be driven only by needs and not wants.

There are two kinds of assets—one whose value appreciates with time and those whose value depreciates over time. As a thumb rule, any asset will depreciate on account of wear and tear due to usage over time. It could also depreciate on account of technological obsolescence. On the other hand, there could be assets whose demand will increase over time—linked to either inflation or a growth in their economic value.

Automobiles and electronic gadgets fall in the category of depreciating assets, while gold and real estate fall in the category of appreciating assets. However, the cost of jewellery design, construction, or interior design lose value over time. In order to both protect and grow your wealth you should allocate your entire surplus wealth towards appreciating assets. Allocation of wealth towards depreciating assets should only be driven by needs and not wants.

For example, mobility, clothing, and housing are legitimate needs of human beings which could be addressed by having one or two cars, a few sets each of formal and casual clothing and a comfortable home to live in. However, splurging on half a dozen luxury cars, dozens of branded suits and footwear, and a home with opulent interiors serves only to feed a person's ego and depreciate his wealth.

You have to bear in mind that spending money on six luxury cars or dozens of suits worth several lakh rupees each only serves to enrich the manufacturers of these products. They signify expenses leading to outflow of your wealth. Their value will keep depreciating every day and you won't be able to recover the wealth that you spent on them. After a few years, their value will fall to zero.

On the other hand, if you had invested your wealth in an appreciating asset, it would have grown and benefitted from the compounding effect that we will discuss in the next chapter.

DEPRECIATING ASSETS AND WHY THEY DEPRECIATE OVER TIME

Depreciating assets are those assets whose economic value falls over time. There are several reasons for this. The most common ones are wear and tear, introduction of better models, launch of new products, or the emergence of new technology that leads to their obsolescence. Consider these examples of everyday life: Do you wear the same clothes and shoes that you did a few years ago? Chances are you do not. Why is that so? Because repeated usage has worn them out. Moreover, they have no resale value. So, you will not be able to monetize them. The only way you can get rid of them is by giving them away to some needy person.

Do you still use a Sony Walkman or an Apple iPod to listen to music while on the move? Again, it is very unlikely you do, except to occasionally feed your sense of nostalgia. These gadgets, which were considered very exclusive and expensive in the 1980s and 2000s, respectively, can now only be found in junk heaps. A few people may still want to retain them for old time's sake, but for the world at large, they have lost all value as technology has marched forward and consumers have moved on to newer, more advanced, and convenient sources of mobile music. This is true of all electronic gadgets.

Even fountain pens, which were such a necessary accessory for anyone who needed to write, are on the way to becoming collectors' items. Most people now use laptops and tablets to type out messages, mails, and memos—that were earlier written in long hand. Likewise, analogue cameras were replaced by digital cameras, which have given way to cameras embedded in smartphones. Automobiles are another example of assets whose value depreciates the moment a new car moves out of the showroom. Though they find buyers in the used car market, it is at a much lower value than the purchase price—depending on various factors like vintage of the model, number of kilometres driven, quality of the maintenance, any accidental damage, residual life, etc.

Furniture and furnishings are other examples of items that could cost a lot of wealth to acquire today. Their value is, however, ephemeral and lies in the perception of the purchaser. In most cases, old furniture and furnishings have no resale value and their worth falls to zero over time. After a few years, they often have to be sold as scrap or given away to needy people for free.

Investing in such depreciating assets is guaranteed to lose you the wealth you spent on acquiring them. Their only return is their utility value, which, too, progressively comes down on account of drop in efficiency due to their usage or technological obsolescence, which renders them useless. With the passage of time there is less and less demand for older generation and used products. This creates a situation where they have no resale market on account of there being no demand for such products or there could be a resale market that is ready to buy such products but only at a steep discount. The situation of either a buyer's market or no market for such products leads to depreciation and, in some cases, complete erosion of the purchase value of such assets. Therefore, you should resist the urge of buying more than your need for such assets as they do not serve any purpose or deliver any value beyond the threshold of your needs. If you do not do that then you simply end up losing the wealth used to acquire such assets which you are never going to use.

APPRECIATING ASSETS AND WHY THEY APPRECIATE OVER TIME

These are assets whose economic value goes up with the passage of time. The key reason for this rise in value is that demand for the assets under consideration is higher than their supply. The primary examples of such assets are gold and real estate. Why is it that these assets see an appreciation in value when others do not? That is because relative demand goes up with time in comparison to supply. Gold reserves are limited. Unlike a crop or a product manufactured in a factory, one cannot grow or manufacture gold in accordance with one's wishes. The demand for gold is driven by usage and has storage value—it is used by central banks around the world and by individuals and investors as a hedge against economic uncertainties and as a safeguard against value erosion due to inflation. Unlike, say oil, which is also a very valuable commodity in the industrial world, its value is not subject to volatility over the long term and it has been used as a storehouse of value since time immemorial across countries and cultures all over the world. If we examine the price behaviour of gold over the past fifty years, we will see that that there are short periods of time when its value stagnates or experiences short-term volatility, but if one considers a longer time horizon of eight to ten years, its value has always shown an appreciation.

Real estate also follows a similar pattern. That is because over a long period of time demand always outstrips supply for a given location. And, as we all know, the real value of real estate lies in its location. For example, a plot of land in a city's central business district or prime residential area will be worth a lot more than a plot of similar dimensions on the outskirts of that city. Advances in engineering technology have given humans the ability to build multi-storied buildings—and this has given more people the ability to enjoy the same plot of land, but there is a threshold beyond which this limit cannot be stretched. Thus, the total supply of land at a given location is capped.

Normal inflation results in the price of that plot of land rising year on year. Then, with rising purchasing power, more people can afford to buy plots and apartments at a given location. The price appreciates as a result of demand outstripping supply.

Let us illustrate this with a concrete example. Let us assume that a plot of land costs ₹100 and the rate of inflation in the economy is 5 per cent. Therefore, all other things remaining constant, the value of that piece of land after one year will be ₹105. Now, let us assume that multiple buyers are interested in buying that plot of land. This will result in the baseline price of that plot of land rising from ₹105 to a higher figure—say

₹110. Then, with time, the infrastructure around that location will get developed, leading to better accessibility and increased facilities in the neighbourhood, making that location sought after by more and more buyers. This process of economic inflation and growth in demand will continue in perpetuity and ensure an appreciation in the value of the land over any reasonable time horizon.

Listed equities is another great example of an appreciating asset. The value of equity of a company appreciates over time and mirrors the growth in the profits of the company. A well-managed company whose business is growing usually earns higher profits with every passing year. This attracts the attention of more and more investors who want to invest in the equity of such a company while the supply of equity available to public investors is limited unless the company issues additional stocks. Rising demand over limited supply of the equity of such companies results in the appreciation of its value over time.

IMPACT OF ALLOCATING WEALTH TO DEPRECIATING ASSETS

When you buy a house, you pay not only for the intrinsic worth of the asset but also spend money on designing the interiors of the house in order to make it habitable in accordance with your taste and budget. Similarly, when you buy gold jewellery, you pay not only for the gold but also a making charge for turning the metal into an ornament.

Both of these are appreciating assets, and you can expect these assets to safeguard the value of your wealth for all time to come. But suppose, in addition to paying ₹1 crore for your house or ₹5 lakh for the gold, you also spend an additional ₹30 lakh on designing the interiors and ₹25,000 as making charges. You will see that though the value of the underlying assets appreciates with time, the amount you spent on interior decoration or making charges will have no resale value. That part of your investment is, therefore, a depreciating asset. Therefore, while investing in a home or buying jewellery one has to be mindful of the allocation of investment towards the appreciating part of the asset, which is the asset itself, and towards the depreciating part of the asset, which is the investment in interiors of the home and the cost of jewellery design and making. As a thumb rule, the allocation towards the depreciating part of the asset should be less than 25 per cent of the overall investment to ensure that the investment delivers returns higher than inflation over a holding period of ten years or more.

Let us take another example. As we have mentioned above, the need for physical mobility is a necessity. So, people buy cars depending on their need and affordability. But you must bear in mind that regardless of what car you buy—whether a Mercedes Benz or a Maruti—its value will depreciate with time. After seven to eight years of usage, its salvage value will be less than 30 per cent of its purchase price. That means, you would have consumed 70 per cent of its value over its useful life of seven to eight years. The same amount of money compounded at a reasonable 10 per cent per annum, on the other hand, would have more than doubled the principal over the same time horizon. It is important to keep this equation in mind when acquiring any high value depreciating asset.

The same holds true for other assets such as watches, or items of high-end clothing, footwear, accessories, or paintings by unknown artists. These might be aesthetically pleasing and might feed your sense of ego but contribute little in terms of adding to your pool of wealth. In fact, they lead to the erosion of your net worth and amounts to a transfer of your wealth to businesses that produce such products for whom the cost of production is a fraction of the sale price of their products.

All these are 'want' products, i.e., they go beyond your needs. The urge to own them is driven by want. Owning them feeds one's ego while the net result on one's wealth is negative in the long term. As we learnt in the previous chapter, anything that fans our ego makes us more and more dependent on external validation and dilutes our self-worth. Accordingly, depreciating assets have a depreciating effect on both our self-worth and net worth.

OPPORTUNITY COST OF INVESTING IN APPRECIATING AND DEPRECIATING ASSETS

The opportunity cost of investing in a depreciating asset over an appreciating asset would be the difference between the respective future values of the appreciating and the depreciating assets if the same amount is invested in each one of them today. It will vary from one depreciating asset to another depending upon the salvage value of the asset in the future. While a few categories of depreciating assets like automobiles and smartphones will have some salvage value, most will not, for the simple reason that there is no resale market for them.

Let us understand this based on the chart below comparing the future value of an appreciating asset like listed equities with different categories of depreciating assets like automobiles, smartphones, interiors, and luxury products like high-end watches, designer clothes, and accessories.

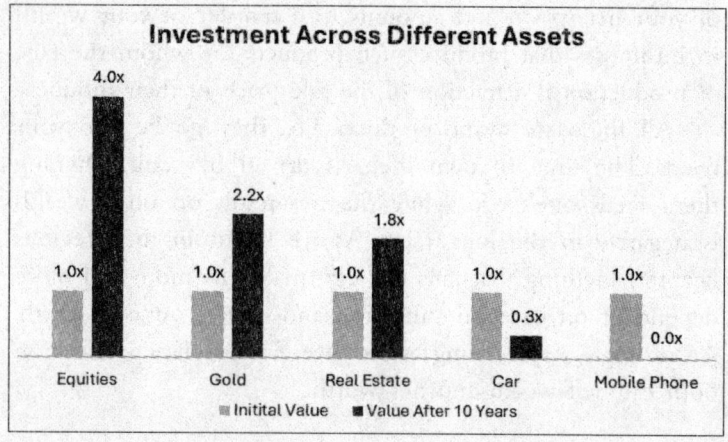

Image 15: Comparison between appreciating and depreciating assets

WEALTH ALLOCATION STRATEGY

It will be clear from the above that a prudent individual will allocate all or most of his/her surplus wealth to appreciating assets. However, as we have discussed in Chapter 14 on Expenses and Lifestyle Management, there is no one-size-fits-all strategy that can satisfy every individual and every situation. For example, some assets have a utility value and provide a return on investment even when their economic value falls. A business owner may want to buy a luxury car more as a business resource than a personal asset. This can lead to opportunities for social mobility enabling wealth creation. In such cases, the acquisition of the depreciating asset becomes an investment that pays dividends over time. Having said that, even in this case while the need for social capital has been met by having one luxury car there is no case for having multiple luxury cars, which would then fall into the category of satisfying wants beyond needs.

Similarly, the Covid-19 pandemic made many people realize that they need bigger homes which meet the requirement of dedicated spaces for a home office, among other things. As a result, many people upgraded to larger homes and spent money doing them up—even though the expenditure on interiors is subject to the laws of depreciating returns. But here too, the focus is on the utility value rather than the intrinsic value of the asset concerned. In this case as well if the wealth gets spent on opulent interiors, it crosses from the zone of the need for having interiors for comfortable and convenient living to the want of living in a palatial home.

As a rule, we must always invest our entire surplus wealth in assets whose value will appreciate with time. The definition of surplus wealth will vary from person to person depending on their individual perception of their needs or must-haves for them and their wants or nice-to-haves for them. However, once the needs are clearly understood it has to be ensured that the decisions for the allocation of wealth are driven by needs and not wants, by self-respect and not ego. While the former help you to keep and compound your wealth as we shall learn in the next chapter, the latter deplete your wealth.

Chapter 17

COMPOUNDING EFFECT REVISITED

The longer you stay invested, the greater is the possibility of growing your wealth. A combination of patience and time is the path to creation and growth of wealth.

We learnt in the previous section how the compounding effect is the driver of wealth creation. It plays an equally important role in growing wealth as well. Time is the foundation of compounding effect and patience is the foundation for both creating and growing wealth. Accordingly, a combination of patience and time is the path to creation and growth of wealth. Once wealth is created, it has to be protected and grown over time for which it needs to be deployed in appreciating assets that stand up well to the vagaries of time.

While the graph of growth in such assets is only upward, the journey in that direction may not be smooth. It requires immense patience to stay invested over a very long time to ride the ups and downs one encounters on the way. It is the time in the market that matters, and not timing the market.

We learnt in Chapter 9 that the compounding effect works by building trust. It is this trust, engendered over long periods of time, that helps build scale. No business or individual can create wealth without scaling up. That is how compounding works in the creation of wealth.

COMPOUNDING AND THE PROTECTION AND GROWTH OF WEALTH

We have also learnt in Chapter 9 that time is the foundation of the compounding effect. Consistent value addition to your stakeholders over a long period of time helps you earn their trust. Your ability to add value to an increasingly larger number of stakeholders like customers and employees helps you scale up and this leads to wealth creation. Likewise, once you have created wealth, time plays a foundational role even in keeping and growing the wealth that has been created. The longer you stay invested, the greater is the benefit of compounding. It will not show results in six months or a year. It takes at least a decade for the compounding effect to start showing significant results.

Try this simple exercise. Use any simple interest calculator and invest a notional amount of ₹100 at, say 10 per cent, for one, two, three, five, ten, and twenty years. Write down your notional gains for each of these time periods. Now, use a compound interest calculator and repeat the exercise. Then, compare the difference in the notional gains for each of the time periods. You will see your gains growing at a faster rate over longer duration of time—the longer you stay invested the more you will benefit from the effect of compounding. For example, if your invested wealth grows at 15 per cent per annum, then it will double every five years becoming 2X, 4X, 8X, 16X, 33X, and 66X at the end of 5, 10, 15, 20, 25, and 30 years, respectively.

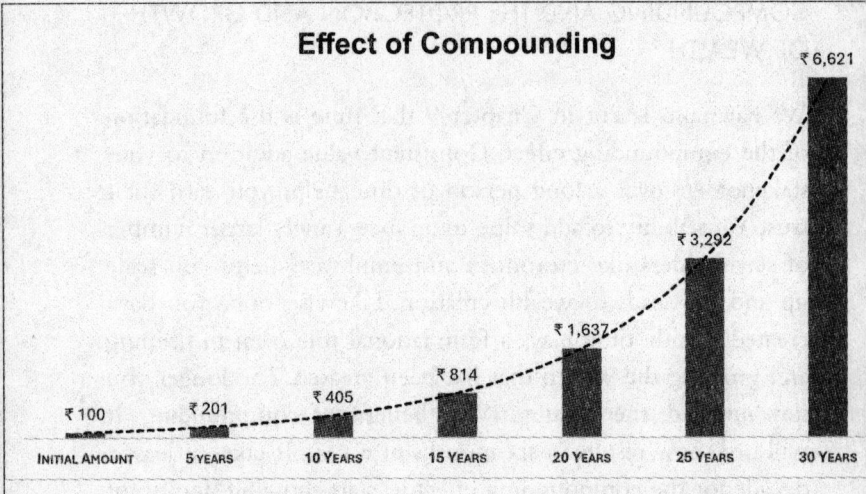

Image 16: The growth of an investment through compounding

ROLE OF TIME AND PATIENCE IN PROTECTING AND GROWING WEALTH

We learnt about the mathematical equation of wealth creation in Chapter 6:

$$FV = PV*(1+R)^N$$

where FV and PV stand for the future value and the present value, respectively, of the investment, while R and N are the rate of return and the time period of the investment.

The future value of your wealth or the effect or output is a function of the cause or the input which is the present value of your wealth growing at a given rate of return over a given time period. In other words, the future value of your wealth invested today is a function of two variables—one, the rate of return at which it grows year on year and two, the number of years it remains invested. The higher the return, the higher will be the future value and likewise, the longer the holding period of your investment, the greater the future value. Between the two, return is a function of the markets and is beyond your control. However, the time you remain invested is your decision entirely. Therefore, if you have the patience to remain invested over a very long period of time you will start reaping the benefits of the compounding effect. The future value of your wealth grown at a relatively lower return over a much longer period of time shall compound to become higher than the future value of your wealth grown at a relatively higher return but over a shorter period of time.

The only way you can remain invested over a long period of time is if you are patient. Time and patience are the two most important variables.

However, while there is a temporal connection between time and patience in general, what is so special about having patience when it comes to compounding your wealth? Long horizon investments—typically between five and twenty years and more—will be subject to lots of volatility. There may be phases along the way when the investments may show a notional loss. For example, there may be stock market crash on account of black swan events like the Global Financial Crisis of 2008, a pandemic like Covid-19 in 2020, or military conflicts like the Russia-Ukraine War in 2022. In the event of such developments, you may see the principal value of your capital fall below its invested value. You will need patience and nerves of steel to stay invested through such periods of unanticipated volatility. If you lose patience and decide to exit your investment, you will convert your notional loss into a real loss.

For example, the BSE Sensex closed on 31 March 2014

at 22,386.27. On 4 February 2024, it closed at 72,085.63. An individual who had invested ₹1,00,000 in the Sensex at the beginning of that period would have grown that to ₹3,22,000 over this period. But the path from 1,00,000 to 3,22,000 has not seen a unidirectional linear progression. There were several ups and downs along the way.

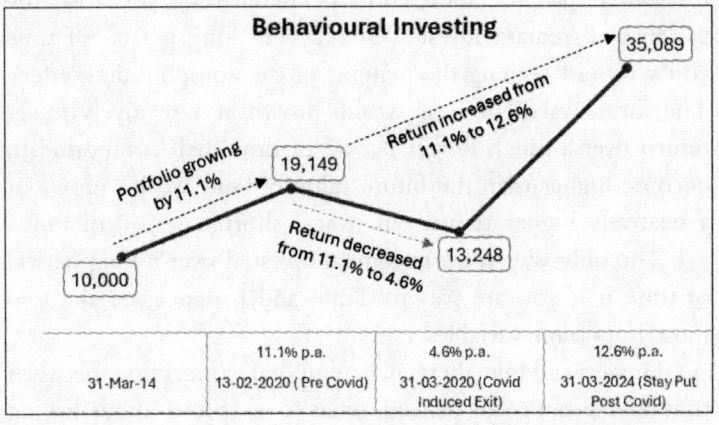

Image 17: The ups and downs in the stock market between March 2014 and March 2024

Covid-19 struck at the beginning of 2020 and the Sensex started crashing from end-February onwards in line with the crash across global equity markets. From a high of 41,500 on 13 February, it fell all the way to 26,000 by 23 March, a massive 37 per cent fall in a matter of forty days. Since fear was the dominant emotion at that time, millions of investors lost their patience and decided to exit the equity markets. This resulted in two outcomes—one, they converted their notional losses into actual losses and two, they completely missed the recovery in the markets. An investor who had invested in the Sensex on 31 March 2014 would have compounded his investment till 13 February 2020 @ almost 11 per cent per annum. However, if he lost patience because of the Covid-19 induced volatility and had exited on 31 March 2020 then his returns would have fallen to a mere 4.5 per cent per annum. Had he stayed the course till February 2024, then the same investment would have compounded at 12.50 per cent per annum.

So, what are the key variables in the mathematical equation of compounding? You must always bear in mind that the rate of return is not under your control. That is market-driven. But the inputs are—the amount you choose to invest and the time horizon of your investment—are under your control. To get the maximum benefit of compounding, you must never let the current returns influence your decision.

Just as creating wealth is about staying in the game and building trust over a long period of time, growing and protecting the wealth is also a function of staying invested over extended periods of time. The same principles apply. Since we are discussing growing the wealth you have already created, it means you have already successfully applied those principles. It is, therefore, a matter of tweaking them slightly to ensure that you retain and continue to grow your wealth.

NUANCES OF THE JOURNEY OF GROWTH IN THE LIFE OF AN APPRECIATING ASSET

Let us examine the journey of two growth asset classes—equities and gold over the last twenty years. The chart below tells us that while each one of them has compounded wealth at their respective growth rates over twenty-five years, they both underwent ups and downs.

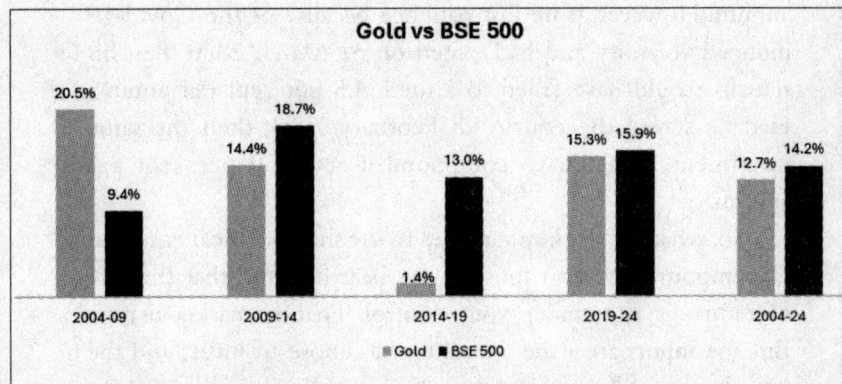

Image 18: Comparison between the growth of gold and the stock market over the past twenty years

The criticality of time and patience in the protection and growth of wealth clearly manifests in the charts above. Only those who stayed invested through the periods of volatility and weathered the storm would have benefitted from the compounding effect. Those who lost patience and exited the market converted their notional losses into real ones and would have probably found it difficult to recoup their losses. The moral of this story is: Never try to time the market; time in the market is always the better and safer option.

THE ADVANTAGES OF THINKING LONG TERM TO HARVEST THE COMPOUNDING EFFECT

Unless you are a market insider, a short-term trading approach will invariably prove to be a hurdle to achieving the compounding effect that we have discussed above.

Why?

According to a publication by the NSE to commemorate

twenty-five years of the Nifty 50 in 2021: 'In terms of calendar year returns between 1999 and 2020, the Nifty 50 TR (total return) index has given positive returns in 17 out of 22 calendar years. Returns were between 0 to 20% in 8 calendar years, 20 to 40% in 5 calendar years and exceeded 40% in 4 calendar years. Out of the 5 calendar years where the Nifty 50 TR index had negative returns, returns were between 0 to -20% in 3 calendar years and less than -20% in 2 calendar years.'

The overall return over this long period was 14.2 per cent. This means, if you had invested ₹1 lakh on the index in 1999, you would have had ₹16,25,505 at the end of that period, an appreciation of more than 1,500 per cent. Most people will find it impossible to match that rate of return on their own.

However, it is important to note that the lip-smacking headline returns figure should not make one oblivious to the fine print. The Nifty 50 generated negative returns in five of these years. If an investor had lost patience and his/her nerve and exited the market as a result of the short-term volatility faced by his portfolio, he would never have benefitted from the cumulative compounding effect by staying invested over the entire twenty-two-year period.

Those with a trading approach are typically driven by the recency bias, and therefore, short-term volatility and price movements play a disproportionately important role in guiding their current investment decisions. But a long-term investor who is keen on compounding his/her wealth knows that the risk of being in the market over a longer term is far lower than the risk of being in and out of it and therefore stays invested to reap the compounding effect.

If, as a result of the recency bias, you sell your portfolio because volatility reduces its value from ₹100 to ₹80, you will never be able to benefit from the rally that will invariably follow when the market recovers and pushes the value of your investment basket to ₹120. The fear of losses will reduce your risk appetite and become an impediment to your journey towards protecting and growing your wealth by harnessing the power of compounding.

Ask any market analyst and he/she will tell you that predicting a long-term trend is easier than forecasting a short-term one. For example, there is enough empirical evidence based on which returns from equities and gold over a period of twenty years could be assumed. However, predicting a thirty-day trend is much more difficult and forecasting what will happen the next day is practically impossible.

Those with a short-term approach to investing are driven more by the emotions of greed and fear and less by merit or logic driven by fundamentals. Their approach is opportunistic. Such an approach invariably results in little or no returns and thereby nil compounding effect. Moreover, such an approach is usually driven by following the crowd while success in investing is all about one's ability to think differently from the crowd. More than the opportunity cost of losing the compounding effect, short-term opportunity driven trading approach could lead to erosion of wealth as well.

Many businesses in the travel sector had to down shutters during Covid-19. But the companies that bet long-term during that trying phase, calculating that the end of the pandemic and a return to normalcy would result in a boom for the travel industry, would have benefitted when the situation did turn around. But here again, only those who had the foresight and resilience to weather the storm would have gained from the boom that followed. Those who exited the business would have lost the opportunity forever.

The moral of the story: The longer you stay invested, the greater is the possibility of growing your wealth. That is the fundamental principle of compounding.

Chapter 18

IMPORTANCE OF FINANCIAL ADVICE

Good financial advisers are no different from successful doctors, lawyers, and architects. Seeking their guidance is essential to protect and grow your wealth.

No matter where we have grown up, we have all experienced the timeless wisdom of the saying—there are no free lunches in life. In fact, the whole rationale of the subject matter of this book on wealth creation is monetization in lieu of value addition. Likewise, there are no free lunches when it comes to seeking financial advice as well. Yet, the investment world is amusingly filled with notions of low cost or even no cost investing, which is the antithesis of wealth creation. Your financial adviser should be your wealth navigator who should guide you on the path of affluence. He/she should not just help you create wealth but, more importantly, keep it throughout your lifetime. The value addition from a good financial adviser is not restricted to knowing what to do but more significantly what not to do.

Readers will appreciate that whenever someone creates wealth, he/she has a new problem to solve—the management, maintenance, and growth of that wealth. The only way to solve this problem is to bring in a specialist to advise on and manage the entire process.

We do consult specialists like doctors, lawyers, and architects when we fall sick, when facing a legal problem, or when designing a house. In most cases, we go to the best professional we can find—and afford. If an individual needs a complicated surgery, he/she will trust only the best team of surgeons to conduct the operation.

The best doctors, iconic lawyers, and the most renowned architects are specialists in their respective domains. They are in greater demand for two reasons—one, the specialist knowledge that they have acquired over decades of their practice and two, their skill to apply this knowledge in a customized manner to each of their patients/clients. Every doctor passes the same set of basic examinations, every lawyer has access to the same set of law books and every architect learns the same design principles when they begin their professional practice. However, it is their ability to build specialization over a long time within their respective domains and then combine that with customization for their target audience that differentiates them within their respective professions making them household names and go-to professionals.

Successful professionals have soft skills like the knack of understanding their client, which allows them to have insight into understanding their expectations and what they want from them as service providers and problem solvers. They are able to customize the delivery of the solution to the problem that their client has in a manner that is aligned to their specific needs. They earn the premium fee that they command. If we entrust the treatment of a loved one to a well-known doctor, we give the patient a greater chance of recovery. If we engage a leading lawyer to represent us in a legal matter, we increase the chances of obtaining a favourable outcome.

In none of the above cases do people think of solving the

medical or legal problems themselves. Yet, when it comes to taking care of their wealth, many people believe they can do it themselves despite having little knowledge of the subject.

Readers can test the veracity of this statement with a simple exercise: Ask people in your social circle—how many of them have made investments based on 'hot tips' from 'people who know'? How many times have you or someone known to you made investments on the basis of a newspaper article or a television discussion—without much additional research to test the validity of those statements or their application to your situation?

Any random sampling will throw up a surprisingly large number of people who will reply in the affirmative—proving that many do not realize the importance of seeking professional advice on wealth management. This approach may have worked to some extent when India's economy was underdeveloped and fixed deposits at banks, real estate, and gold were the most preferred savings instruments.

But with the growth of the Indian economy and its integration with the world, people have many more avenues to park their wealth. Apart from the old favourites mentioned above, investors now have the choice of various vehicles like mutual funds, exchange traded funds, portfolio management schemes (PMS), alternative investment funds (AIFs), and real estate investment trusts (REITS) to invest in a diverse set of asset classes—venture capital, private equity, listed equities, private credit, debt alternatives, real estate, and gold. It is also possible to access these opportunities outside India to achieve geographical, economic, and currency diversification.

Such a diverse portfolio across multiple asset classes, vehicles, fund managers, investment strategies, and geographies requires domain expertise and active management. It needs specialist knowledge to construct an efficient portfolio across all these parameters in order to achieve the desired financial goal of growing the wealth at a given growth rate within acceptable levels of risk. However, constructing the portfolio is only the beginning of the journey of managing wealth efficiently. Actively managing the portfolio on an ongoing basis in the context of an everchanging market and economic environment is a lifelong journey of protecting and growing wealth.

But access to such domain expertise and active management comes at a price much like any other specialists. While selecting a doctor or a lawyer, you will not only look at the fee. You will look at competence, track record, and reputation to help you select the right specialist. Choosing the lowest cost doctor or lawyer can lead to an unfortunate outcome that could prove to be more expensive in the long run. Similarly, high quality advice for managing wealth also comes at a price. Since there are no free lunches in life, we should be willing to pay this price to do justice to our hard-earned wealth.

Good advice does not come at low cost—and it certainly does not come free.

WHY FINANCIAL ADVICE IS REQUIRED

Ownership of wealth comes with the responsibility of taking care of it. Once you create wealth you have to manage it well. Your wealth secures your life financially and is the resource that enables you to live the life that you desire. If the scale of your wealth is large enough to last beyond your lifetime, then it also becomes your legacy, which then has to be protected for the benefit of future generations.

In addition, once you become a wealth owner you invite

emotions of greed and fear. Your opportunity cost—between good and poor decisions—goes up since the divergence between optimal and unsatisfactory outcomes could be much greater. The stakes are much higher as you have something to lose. At the same time, you can grow wealth faster, overcoming the fear and greed that invariably come into play.

If you have a large corpus of wealth that can last beyond your lifetime, you have to be extra careful in safeguarding the legacy you have created. How you manage and grow the wealth that you have created will affect you and your descendants. This implies a much higher stake in managing and growing your wealth and makes it imperative for you to have good financial advice to help you overcome the emotions of fear and greed that invariably come into play in such situations. This adviser will help you avoid emotional and irrational decisions thereby helping you to compound your wealth over your lifetime.

As we saw in Chapter 4, adding value is a foundational law of wealth creation. Your financial adviser as your wealth navigator adds value by enabling you to protect and grow your wealth over your lifetime. A prudent wealth owner will allow himself/herself to be guided by such a professional on the path of wealth management.

HOW A FINANCIAL ADVISER ADDS VALUE

Does a financial adviser help you earn better returns or give you a better quality of life—enabling you to focus on your strengths and have peace of mind? What is the real value of a financial adviser?

Just because you have created wealth does not mean you are also good at managing it. It is a specialist skill and may not be your area of strength. For example, you may be more inclined towards creation of wealth and less enamoured by its maintenance. That is why high-net-worth individuals all over the world engage the services of professional wealth managers to manage their wealth while they focus on their primary calling of creating more of it.

For example, a doctor, a lawyer, a sportsperson, or even a businessman may be very good at creating wealth from their primary profession. However, they may not have the willingness and the ability to manage their wealth. A competent financial adviser will bring value in terms of quantitative benefits that can help them grow their wealth not just faster than what they could do on their own but more importantly, in line with their desired goals. This financial adviser could also bring immense value in terms of qualitative benefits. He can help these professionals disengage from the management of their wealth, which then no longer remains a source of distraction from their core strength of creating wealth in their profession. Delegation of the management of wealth to a financial adviser bestows peace of mind to the wealth owner while at the same time giving him/her the freedom to pursue what he/she enjoys the most. Therefore, peace of mind and joy are two intangible and priceless benefits which a good financial adviser could bring in the life of a wealth owner.

THE VALUE A GOOD FINANCIAL ADVISER BRINGS

How can you tell if your financial adviser is giving you good advice? In the previous section we have examined the ways in which a good financial adviser adds value. One was in terms of the rate of return at which he/she grows your wealth. This part of the value addition is tangible and, therefore, can be quantified in various ways. One of the simplest ways to make this assessment is to see if your financial adviser is able to grow your wealth faster than the returns generated by the market of the underlying asset classes you are invested in. This excess return over the relevant market/asset class benchmark is called 'alpha' in the investment management industry and is an established measure of performance or underperformance. For example, if the BSE Sensex has given a return of 12 per cent compounded every year over a period of ten years and your portfolio, invested in a diversified mix of listed equities under the guidance of your financial adviser, has grown at 15 per cent every year during the same period, then the excess return or alpha of 3 per cent every year is the value addition of your financial adviser. There is enough empirical evidence that the value addition by a good financial adviser could be 2-3 per cent per annum on the equity portfolio and 1-2 per cent per annum at the overall portfolio level, which includes other asset classes like debt and alternatives.

We must bear in mind that there are several years when the BSE Sensex (or any other proxy for the market) will give negative returns. For example, it may lose 10 per cent in a given year. In such a loss-making year, a good financial adviser may not be able to grow your wealth, but he/she should be able to keep your losses lower than that suffered by the broader market.

There is another more significant way in which the value addition of a financial adviser can be understood. Empirical evidence suggests that people who are not regular investors in the market tend to lose patience and their nerve when prices correct, and pull out of the investment. A good financial adviser is truly a financial counsellor who handholds you and helps you stay invested by navigating the volatile times in the markets. He/she helps you take rational decisions that guard you against the pitfalls of the herd mentality. He/she will help you stay invested when everyone is fearful and exiting the market. He/she will also stop you from increasing your exposure when valuations are expensive, and you see everyone buying based on lucrative returns over the past twelve months. There is enough empirical evidence that tells us that value addition of a good financial adviser on this count is the largest and could range anywhere from 3-5 per cent per annum in the case of an equity portfolio.

CHOOSING A FINANCIAL ADVISER

If you are looking for a doctor to treat a serious health condition, would you go for the lowest cost medical practitioner you can find? Chances are you will not. Similarly, it will not make sense to entrust your wealth—your financial security and legacy—to the lowest cost financial adviser in the wealth management industry.

Let us take an example. Fund A gives 10 per cent returns and charges 1 per cent as management fees. So, an investor in this fund gets a net return of 9 per cent. Fund B, on the other hand, gives 15 per cent returns but charges 2 per cent as management fees. Which one will you choose?

A rational individual will choose Fund B despite the higher fees of 2 per cent it charges because the net returns of 13 per cent are higher than the returns delivered by lower cost Fund A. The rational objective will be to choose a fund not with the lowest fee but the highest post-fee returns.

This simple example illustrates that when it comes to financial advice, cheap is usually more expensive.

You should find a financial adviser who has an established track record of adding value by way of documented alpha creation over at least ten years if not more, has a reputation to protect, and whose key core values match with yours. Most wealth owners may not realize that the real cost of financial advice is not what they pay their financial adviser but actually the returns which they do not earn on account of poor advice since that part is often invisible to them. There could be a case where a financial adviser is charging a relatively low fee to keep the business but is underperforming on the portfolio significantly. Therefore, while the wealth owner could be gaining by paying a lower fee, he/she could be losing much more because of the missed growth opportunities. Like all other professional services, good financial advice also comes at a price. The objective of every wealth owner then should be to engage a good financial adviser as their long-term wealth navigator who will help them grow their wealth at the best possible returns.

CONCLUSION

A Quick Guide to the Laws of Creating, Protecting, and Growing Wealth

We have looked at the various rules and formulae for creating, protecting, and growing wealth. Let us go over the most important aspects:

- Wealth is the fuel that plays a critical role in harnessing a country's true potential. It is the life force behind national, social, and individual well-being. Creating wealth and generating surplus should be considered a mandatory obligation of every member of society.
- Access to wealth gives you control over your life. It also enables you, the wealth creator, to positively impact society by spreading prosperity either by giving back or inspiring others to become wealth creators.
- You can become a successful wealth creator by equipping yourself with the relevant skills and knowledge, adapting to your circumstances, making optimal use of your resources, having the hunger to reach your goal and the stomach to absorb the risk as you get there. You must also have the ability to learn new things, the capacity for hard work, and a dogged determination to overcome obstacles.
- One person's expense is another person's income. That is how wealth gets created. Every product or service

solves some problem of the society for which the society is willing to pay a price. That is the beginning of the wealth creation process.

- Hunger is the pursuit of growth with wealth creation as its by-product. It is a positive attribute driven by the larger goal of lifting the entire ecosystem. Greed is the pursuit of wealth itself which often leads to its unequal distribution. Hunger and greed can both lead to wealth creation in the short term. However, an individual driven by hunger is better placed to be a perpetual wealth creator while one fuelled by greed will eventually lose his/her wealth.
- There is a cause-and-effect relationship between effort or input and reward or output. The desired outcomes—or output—follow required inputs—this is the law of karma at work—in life and in the field of wealth creation.
- If a business is driven by its larger purpose defined by its positive impact on the society, that becomes its perennial source of energy which keeps it ever relevant. Pursuit of scale while ignoring the purpose of the business eventually leads to its attrition and therefore erosion of wealth.
- There is a linear relationship between risk and reward. Measured decision-making can help optimize risk for a given reward, whereas poor decision making can lead to no reward and even loss. Judiciously addressed, risk taking is the path to wealth creation.
- When you solve problems for society with consistency over a long period of time, you develop into a dependable brand. This bond of trustworthiness between you and society attracts more work, leading

to wealth creation. This is the compounding effect at work where small, incremental, and consistent effort over long periods of time results in big outcomes.
- Wealth creation is all about constant evolution, adaptation, and on-the-job learning. Rare is the successful entrepreneur who has never failed in any venture or a successful investor who hasn't lost money. Success and failure teach us to learn from experience of what works and what does not.
- Wealth creation is the by-product of doing what needs to be done when it needs to be done. Only those who show up and work hard are able to reach the top of their craft.
- In order to retain wealth, it needs to be actively managed. The resources required to safeguard wealth are very different from those that went into its creation.
- Protecting wealth ensures that its principal value remains intact at all times, whereas growth increases the principal value by allowing it to compound over time. One must learn to strike a balance between the two.
- Lifestyle inflation is a bigger threat to wealth erosion than financial inflation. So lifestyle management becomes critical to retaining wealth.
- Recognition comes from two sources—internal and external. When it is external it is called ego; and when it is internal, we call it self-respect. Decisions driven by ego could be irrational leading to erosion of wealth. Individuals with awareness of self-worth usually have greater reserves of humility which helps them to remain grounded. Therefore, self-management is the bedrock of wealth management.
- Most assets depreciate over time. There are some assets

whose demand increases over time. Spending your wealth on depreciating assets should be driven only by needs and not wants.
- The compounding effect is the driver of wealth creation and plays a very important role in protecting and growing wealth. A combination of patience and time is the path to the creation and growth of wealth.
- Once you create wealth, you have to manage, maintain, and grow that wealth. To do this, you must also seek out expert advice from a financial adviser with an established track record.

ACKNOWLEDGEMENTS

It has always been my core belief that no one in this world is self-made. Whatever one achieves, big or small, is the result of the contributions of numerous stakeholders around us. We are only the recipients of the blessings of the universe in response to our actions.

The project of *Unlocking Wealth* too has been an outcome of the nudges, belief, encouragement, and action of several individuals that I am so blessed and privileged to have in my life. It begins with my extended family of colleagues at Client Associates who made me believe over the years that there is a book inside me and I must work on it. With these nudges came the encouragement from David Davidar, Publisher, Aleph Book Company, who thought that I was ready to be an author. When someone as credible as David, who has published the leading lights of the literary world tells you this, you have to start believing that you can do it.

During the course of writing the book I received invaluable help from my colleagues from our Investment Research team at Client Associates in gathering and analysing the data to derive the key takeaways essential to validate my own understanding of the subject of wealth. While Rohit Kumar helped me pull and analyse the data, Paul Nicholas helped me to convey the takeaways graphically. These are our data scientists who filter truth from numbers. Pujitha Krishnan, editor at Aleph, at the beginning of the project helped me conceptualize and structure the book. Towards the end she helped to give the book the polish of a professional author which was much needed for a first-time author. Her work tells me clearly why she does what she does since she is so good at it. I would also like to thank Aarnab Mitra for his valuable guidance in writing the book.

Lastly, it is my family which contributed right from the opening to the last mile to the accomplishment of this project. Picking up duties ahead of rights and excellence in whatever you do has been the core of my upbringing. I don't think I could have delivered on this project without the foundation of these values. It took me seven months with at least five hours of family time every week to put this book together. I don't think I could have even attempted to put in this effort without the backing and love of my family.

I shall remain eternally grateful to all stakeholders as co-creators of this book. This book is dedicated to your vision, belief, and effort. Thank you for being around and making this reality. There was only so much that I could have done on my own.

REFERENCES

Image 1: Bloomberg

Image 2: Bloomberg

Image 3: Bloomberg

Image 4: 'About the Endowment', Harvard University, Harvard.edu, available at <https://www.harvard.edu/about/endowment/>; 'Yale Investments Office', Yale University, Yale.edu, available at <https://investments.yale.edu/>; 'Endowment Continues to Support Princeton's Commitment to Affordability, Excellence in Teaching', Princeton University, Princeton.edu, available at <https://www.princeton.edu/news/2023/10/25/endowment-continues-support-princetons-commitment-affordability-excellence-teaching>; 'IMC CEO Statement on FY23 Endowment Returns', Columbia University, Columbia.edu, available at <https://www.finance.columbia.edu/content/imc-ceo-statement-fy23-endowment-returns#:~:text=The%20total%20value%20of%20Columbia's,the%20endowment%20in%20fiscal%202023.>; 'Endowment', Brown University, Brown.edu, available at <https://investment.brown.edu/endowment; 'Dartmouth Reports Endowment Return for Fiscal 2023', Dartmouth College, Dartmouth.edu, available at <https://home.dartmouth.edu/news/2023/10/dartmouth-reports-endowment-return-fiscal-2023>; 'About Us', University of Pennsylvania, UPenn.edu, available at <https://investments.upenn.edu/about-us>; 'University Endowment Reports Solid Return for FY 2023',

Cornell University, Cornell.edu, available at <https://news.cornell.edu/stories/2023/10/university-endowment-reports-solid-return-fy-2023>.

Image 5: 'GDP per Capita (Current US$)', World Bank, WorldBank.org, available at <https://data.worldbank.org/indicator/NY.GDP.PCAP.CD>; 'Worldwide Governance Indicators', World Bank, WorldBank.org, available at <https://www.worldbank.org/en/publication/worldwide-governance-indicators>.

Image 6: 'Handbook of Statistics on Indian States', Reserve Bank of India, RBI.org, available at <https://www.rbi.org.in/Scripts/AnnualPublications.aspx?head=Handbook+of+Statistics+on+Indian+States>.

Image 7: 'Handbook of Statistics on Indian States', Reserve Bank of India, RBI.org, available at <https://www.rbi.org.in/Scripts/AnnualPublications.aspx?head=Handbook+of+Statistics+on+Indian+States>.

Image 8: 'Handbook of Statistics on Indian States', Reserve Bank of India, RBI.org, available at <https://www.rbi.org.in/Scripts/AnnualPublications.aspx?head=Handbook+of+Statistics+on+Indian+States>.

Image 9: 'Handbook of Statistics on Indian States', Reserve Bank of India, RBI.org, available at <https://www.rbi.org.in/Scripts/AnnualPublications.aspx?head=Handbook+of+Statistics+on+Indian+States>.

Image 10: 'The Two Germanies: Planning and Capitalism', Our World in Data, OurWorldInData.org, available at <https://ourworldindata.org/grapher/the-two-germanies-planning-and-capitalism>; 'Population of East and West Germany', Statista, Statista.com, available at <https://www.

statista.com/statistics/1054199/population-of-east-and-west-germany/#:~:text=During%20the%20German%20partition%2C%20the,16.4%20million%20during%20this%20time.>.

Image 11: 'Fortune 500 Archive', *CNN Money*, available at <https://money.cnn.com/magazines/fortune/fortune500_archive/full/1955/1.html>; 'Fortune 500', 50Pros, 50Pros.com, available at <https://www.50pros.com/fortune500>.

Image 15: For Equities, we have used BSE 500's performance as of April'24 from *Bloomberg*; For Gold and Real Estate, RBI's Housing Price Index ('Housing Price Index', Reserve Bank of India, RBI.org, available at <https://cimsdbie.rbi.org.in/DBIE/#/dbie/home>); For Cars, we have assumed it is depreciating at 10%, at this rate it's salvage value would be 30% in 10 years; For Mobile Phones, we have assumed it is depreciating at 30%, at this rate it's salvage value would be ~0% in 10 years.

Image 17: Bloomberg

Image 18: For Equities, we have used BSE 500's performance as of April'24 from *Bloomberg*; For Gold, RBI's Housing Price Index ('Housing Price Index', Reserve Bank of India, RBI.org, available at <https://cimsdbie.rbi.org.in/DBIE/#/dbie/home>).